The Confederacy
Is on Her Way
Up the Spout

The Confederacy
Is on Her Way
Up the Spout

LETTERS TO
SOUTH CAROLINA,
1861–1864

EDITED BY

J. Roderick Heller III
and
Carolynn Ayres Heller

Foreword by James M. McPherson

UNIVERSITY OF SOUTH CAROLINA PRESS

© 1998 by J. Roderick Heller III

First cloth edition published 1992 by the

University of Georgia Press

First paperback edition published 1998 by

the University of South Carolina Press

Printed in the United States of America

02 01 00 99 98   5 4 3 2 1

Library of Congress Cataloging-in-Publication Data

The Confederacy is on her way up the spout : letters to South
Carolina, 1861–1864 / edited by
J. Roderick Heller III and Carolynn Ayers Heller.
p. cm.
A collection of 33 letters, written by Milton Barrett
and six other Confederate soldiers.
Originally published: Athens : University of Georgia Press, c1992.
Includes bibliographical references and index.
ISBN 1-57003-254-8 (pbk.)
1. South Carolina—History—Civil War, 1861–1865—Personal
narratives. 2. Soldiers—South Carolina—Correspondence. 3. United
States—History—Civil War, 1861–1865—Personal narratives,
Confederate.   I. Heller, J. Roderick (John Roderick), 1937–   .
II. Heller, Carolynn Ayres.   III. Barrett, Milton, b. 1827 or 8.
[E605.C74   1998]
973.7'82—DC21   97-41116

TO THE MEMORY OF
Milton Barrett, CSA

"*He was a good soldier and was always
at his Post both in camp and in the time of battle.*"

Contents

Foreword

The letters of Civil War soldiers are among the richest of sources for American history. They exist in great abundance. Civil War armies were the most literate in history to that time. Three million men, Union and Confederate, went away from home for extended periods, many for the first time in their lives. Aware that they were engaged in a great venture, they wrote home frequently, describing their experiences and feelings. Their letters, unlike those of soldiers in later wars, were not subject to censorship. Thus they wrote about all sorts of things with candor and pungency: their marches and battles, their officers, politicians, the conduct and issues of the war, the wisdom or foolishness of military operations, and so on. These letters offer an unmatched perspective on the war from the viewpoint of the men who fought it. Because the soldiers were hungry for news from home, and because most of the men in each company came from the same town or county, their letters also focus on community affairs in a manner that opens a window for an unparalleled view of American social and cultural life in the mid nineteenth century.

The letters in *The Confederacy Is On Her Way Up the Spout*, mainly from three brothers and one brother-in-law who served as enlisted men in the Confederate army, yield tantalizing glimpses of Southern mores and Confederate military affairs. Yeoman farmers from up-country South Carolina and Georgia, they had a meager education that manifested itself in the creative spelling and imaginative grammar of these letters. But they had no problem describing their experiences at the fighting fronts in Virginia, Tennessee, and North and South Carolina in graphic terms. Many themes of the Civil War experience come alive in piquant, succinct prose.

THE DEDICATION of Confederate soldiers to "the cause": "you must show this letter to mother an tel hear not to be uneasy about me but to be proud rather than serow that she has two sons engage in the cose of ther cuntry and if you toment a tall let hit be be cose you have not twenty engage in the glouris cose."

THE LIMITED PERSPECTIVE of a private: "hit is all ways expected of those at home when tha git a letter from a solger in serves to hear all that is a going on in the armey but hit is a mis stake. a sholger nows but litle moar what is a goin on than you do only in his own ridge ment or when he receves orders to march and than he dont know whether hit is for a fight or to change en campements til he sees the enmey."

THE QUALITY AND QUANTITY of rations: "we have bicets that is so hard i could nock a bull down with one." "Tha curtail down our rashings to two thirds of a pound of flour not bolted and ⅓ a pound of bacon. This cose grate dissadisfaction a mong the soldiers. in fack it was barley enuf for one meal per day. Hungry will cose a man to do all most any thing. Tha was severil depperdation committed on the sittuzins property sutch as taken chickens and meat. The thing went on this way for several days, the men all hungry and mad."

THE JOYS of camping out in all kinds of weather: "the rain continud to fall an the wind increast. by midnight our tents was blowed down an every thing rining wet and the earth so soft and the wind a bloing we could not get our tents to stand."

THE ATTITUDE of Confederate soldiers toward black Union troops, implied in this chilling account of the battle of the Crater in which Confederates captured many white Union troops but deliberately shot blacks trying to surrender: "Our troops charged them, got back to the works, killed five hundred negroes and took two prisoners and set them to work. We took 1,000 white troops."

Most of the letters published here are from Milton Barrett, a soldier in the Eighteenth Georgia, Longstreet's Corps. Many passages in his letters convey a sense of "you are there" to the reader, as in this sentence in the middle of one letter: "the Yankees is advancen i must lay down my pen and go to shooting."

These letters constitute a microcosm of Confederate history. Their mood deteriorates from jaunty confidence in 1861–62 to war weariness and defeatism in 1863–64. And their quantity diminishes from thirteen letters in the first year of the war to only two in the last year, as Union invasion disrupted communications and Southerners suffered growing shortages of everything, including paper. But the most significant reason for the decrease of letters is the death of each of the three Barrett brothers and their brother-in-law as the war dragged on. The destruction of this family mirrors the destruction of the Confederacy and the way of life for which they fought.

J. Roderick Heller III and his daughter Carolynn Ayres Heller, collateral descendants of the soldiers whose letters are published in this volume, have done a skillful job of deciphering and editing the letters and of supplying just the right amount of historical context and commentary to enrich the reader's understanding of them. To comprehend the nature of the "real war," which Walt Whitman said would "never get into the books," we need to get beneath the artificial symmetry of narrative histories, of neat lines and arrows on battle maps, of command decisions and orders from headquarters, to the human dimensions of the conflict. And there is no better place to start than with the letters in this volume.

JAMES M. MCPHERSON

Preface

The letters from the Confederate soldiers in this volume were written from 1861 to 1864 to Jesse McMahan and Lucretia Caroline Barrett McMahan of Pickens County, South Carolina. They were preserved by Lucretia and now are widely scattered among Lucretia's descendants, of whom we are two.

We decided to compile and publish these thirty-three letters for more than antiquarian interest. We wished to preserve the record of how seven soldiers viewed and fought a war in which most of them perished. More important, we hoped that the letters would provide insight into why the Southern yeoman farmer went so enthusiastically to war for a system at the heart of which were slaves he would probably never own. We also were interested in whether inhabitants of these mountainous counties had Unionist sentiments, similar to those of their kin in east Tennessee.

The letters shed much less light than we had hoped on why these soldiers went to war. This result is perhaps not surprising. As many of the soldiers were away from home for the first time, the letters were written as descriptions of faraway places and events. In addition, these soldiers were not writing for posterity, but to keep in touch with family members and friends. These unanalytical letters, in fact, probably better reflect the average Confederate soldier's outlook than do those diaries or letters that reveal more studied perspectives. Indeed, the explanation for enlistments ultimately may be found in such everyday factors as the boredom of farm life, community pressure, and the lure of glory and excitement.

Even though the letters reveal little about why these soldiers went to war, they proved to be of considerable historical interest. Twenty of the thirty-three letters are from Milton Barrett, who served with the Eighteenth Georgia from his enlistment on June 13, 1861, until his capture on August 16, 1864. The Eighteenth Georgia was part of the Texas Brigade, one of the great fighting units of the Confederacy, until after Antietam. Barrett, moreover, proved to be a regular correspondent, and his letters provide the unique perspective of an ordinary soldier throughout most of the war. We know of few other collections of letters from a Confederate foot soldier covering such a long period of time.

Perhaps more important, the letters offer an opportunity to explore how the Civil War affected an up-country South Carolina family over four years. The yeoman farm family only recently has become the subject of detailed scrutiny, and such brilliant studies as Lacy K. Ford, Jr.'s *Origins of Southern Radicalism: The South Carolina Upcountry, 1800–1860* have added significantly to our knowledge of the "plain folk" of the Confederacy. Information on yeoman families, however, generally remains sparse. These letters, combined with the available background material on the Barretts, thus bring partially to light the responses of the members of one yeoman farm family to the creation of the Confederacy and reveal the ultimately devastating effect of the war on them.

The Confederacy
Is on Her Way
Up the Spout

Introduction

The area that became Pickens District, South Carolina, was settled rapidly after it was wrested from the Cherokees during the American Revolution. Pendleton District, comprising the future Anderson, Oconee, and Pickens counties, was formed in 1789. Pendleton became an important way station for families from Virginia and North Carolina moving to Georgia and states further west. Many families, however, principally of English and Scots-Irish descent, stayed in the rolling region at the foothills of the Appalachian Mountains.

Pickens District was created in 1826 when Pendleton District was divided into Pickens and Anderson districts. By 1860 Pickens, consisting of the present Oconee and Pickens counties in the northwest corner of the state, was composed of relatively small tracts of land held by yeoman farmers. William Barrett owned a farm of approximately one hundred acres on Georges Creek. He and his wife, Mary Bradley Barrett, were the parents of Milton, Lawrence, and Benjamin Barrett, whose letters are featured in this study.

The origins of the Barrett and Bradley families are obscure. They appear to have been of English descent and may well have traced their ancestry to early settlers in Virginia. The Barrett and Bradley families were neighbors in Pickens District and could have been continuing a pattern set in North Carolina. In 1779 Margaret Barrett, Lawrence

Bradley, Ambrose Bradley, Elisha Hammond, and William and George Archer were in Randolph County, North Carolina, and all would settle near each other in up-country South Carolina. Margaret, who was still in Randolph County in 1790, may have been the mother of Thomas Barrett.

Thomas Barrett, grandfather of our Confederate letter writers, acquired the farm subsequently owned by his son William. Thomas apparently was born during the revolutionary period (between 1765 and 1784) and first appears in the records of Pendleton District on February 16, 1799, when he purchased one hundred acres on Georges Creek from Thomas Boyd. Thomas Barrett's wife was named Mary and, from census records, appears to have been born between 1784 and 1789.

Thomas and Mary Barrett had at least two sons, William and Benjamin, and four daughters. Thomas apparently died before 1820. Mary Barrett may have lived until the Civil War; 1860 census records show Mary Barrett, aged seventy-five, living near the farm of Lawrence Barrett.

William Barrett was born in 1798 or 1799 in South Carolina and married Mary Bradley in 1825. Mary was born in 1804, the youngest child of Lawrence Bradley, a farmer who was born between 1765 and 1774 and who died before 1820. Lawrence apparently was reasonably prosperous, farming at least three hundred acres.

William and Mary Barrett had at least four sons and five daughters who lived to maturity. William died on June 12, 1859, his will being executed ten days before his death. At the beginning of the Civil War, less than two years after William Barrett's death, the Barrett family consisted of the widow and her nine children. The oldest child was Lucretia Caroline, born on April 5, 1826. She had married Jesse

McMahan on February 26, 1848, at Carmel Presbyterian Church. Jesse McMahan, the son of a revolutionary war soldier, was significantly older than his bride, having been born on July 15, 1804. By 1860 Jesse and Lucretia McMahan had six children, the oldest of whom, Laurana, was already eleven; two more sons were to be born during the war, and one in 1867.

The second child in the Barrett family was Milton, who was born in 1827 or 1828. He married Malissa Durham but, according to family records, was subsequently divorced. At the time of the war he was living in Georgia, apparently in Acworth, but we have found no information indicating when he moved to that state. Rebecca Emeline, the third child, was born in 1829 and married James McCoy. She had four children and resided in Pickens County. The fourth child and second son was Benjamin Barrett, born in 1830 or 1831. He married Martha Ann Gibson. Mary Ann, the sixth child, was born in 1839 and married John Powers shortly after her father's death in 1859. In 1860 Mary Ann was living with her husband's family and her son, Joseph E. (one month old when the census was taken), in Spartanburg District. Interestingly, Mary Ann was listed in 1860 as having attended school within the past year.

Living at the home farm on Georges Creek in 1860, then, were Mary Barrett, fifty-six, and her four unmarried children: William Lawrence, born in 1832 and apparently the mainstay of the family; Sarah Jane, born in 1841; Malinda P., born in 1843; and John Henry, born in 1849.

The Barrett family did not live in isolation, but as part of an interconnected network of friends and family. Steven Hahn, in his book *The Roots of Southern Populism*, refers to settlement patterns in Georgia in terms equally applicable to South Carolina. He notes that "settlers normally migrated with neighbors or kin, partly to mitigate the hardships, dangers, and loneliness of frontier life. At times, they were bound together by religious or ethnic ties. . . . Families seemed particularly inclined to locate near one another. At least a quarter of the farmers in any district, in fact, would have one or more neighboring relatives."[1]

This pattern certainly fit the Barretts. We have already seen that in 1779 Bradley, Barrett, and Archer families were living near each other in North Carolina; not coincidentally, these same families were neighbors in Pickens County in 1860. In addition, the Barrett children appear to have been reared in a large household of relatives. In the 1840 census, for example, the William Barrett household included four female members over age thirty and only one male in that age category. In the 1860 census, the household listed as next to Mary Barrett's consisted of Ruth Barrett, sixty-two, and Sarah Barrett, fifty-five. Mary Barrett, seventy-five, and Rebecca Barrett, forty, were nearby neighbors, along with Jesse and Lucretia McMahan and various Bradleys and McMahans. References to the McMahan, Archer, King, and Mauldin families are made in several letters in this collection. In short, the Barrett soldiers were part of a group connected by blood and neighborhood.

William Barrett's will provides some insight into the economic circumstances of his family. His farm consisted of a hundred acres "on a prong of Georges Creek waters of Saluda River" and was bounded by the lands of Malinda Archer and William King, among others. William Barrett left the land to his wife, Mary; other than one cow and one bed left to each of his three unmarried daughters, William left the remainder of his estate, "share and share alike" to his nine children. Property specifically referred to in the will included one bay horse, five head of cattle, eight head of hogs, and a one-horse wagon and harness. Estate records suggest that the principal cash crop of the farm was cotton.

The agricultural schedules of the 1860 census provide more detailed information on the Barrett farm. Mary Barrett's 100-acre tract included 80 improved and 20 unimproved acres, with the farm accorded a cash value of $700. The farm produced 5 bushels of peas and beans, 40 bushels of sweet potatoes, 30 pounds of butter, 5 pounds of beeswax, and 15 pounds of honey. More important, the farm also produced 130 bushels of Indian corn and a wide variety of other products, including sugar, flax, flax seed, hemp, hops, hay, clover seed, and cheese.

Some neighboring farms were larger and more valuable. Malinda Archer, for example, had a farm of 200 improved acres and 400 unimproved acres with a value of $4,000. In the Arnold's Mills area of Pickens District where the Barretts lived, 27 of the 31 farms were accorded a higher value than the Barrett farm. Jesse McMahan, married to Lucretia Caroline Barrett, had only 50 improved acres, but he owned 175 unimproved acres, and his total farm was valued at $1,000. Benjamin Mauldin and William King had farms of about the same size and value as the Barrett farm.

Taken as part of the Upper Piedmont area (Pickens, Anderson, Greenville, Spartanburg, York, and Lancaster counties), the Barrett farm appears representative. Lacy K. Ford, Jr., in his book *Origins of Southern Radicalism*, states that 60 percent of all farms in every district except York contained no more than a hundred improved acres, and nearly one-third of all farms contained no more than fifty improved acres.[2]

Slaveholding was fairly widely distributed throughout South Carolina, as many commentators have stressed in reviewing the strength of the secession movement in the state. Census records show that in 1860, however, Pickens District had the second lowest slave population in South Carolina in absolute numbers and the fewest slaves relative to the total population (21 percent). The Pickens District ratio of slaves to free white population, 4,195 to 15,335, contrasted sharply with the statewide total of 402,606 slaves to 291,300 whites. Even in the Upper Piedmont, where small farms dominated, Pickens stood out as a stronghold of the yeoman farmer.

Pickens District was not excluded from the economic growth experienced by the rest of the South in the decade preceding the Civil War. The 1850s was the boom time for growing cotton, and there was significant expansion of cotton production throughout the state, including the Upper Piedmont. Ford notes that subsistence farming remained the norm in the Upper Piedmont but experienced a relative decline as more and more production was shifted to cotton. Some evidence of this is seen in census figures for Pickens District, reflecting the growth in the number of slaves. In 1840 the total population was 14,356, of which 1,459 (10 percent) were slaves. By 1860 the total population was 19,665, including 135 free blacks, but 4,195 (21 percent) were slaves.

The 1850s also saw a great increase in railroads, which of course facilitated export of cotton from the up-country. In 1848 there was only one railroad in South Carolina, operating 248 miles of track; by 1860 there were eleven railroads and nearly 1,000 miles of track.[3] Not all areas benefited from the railroad, however. While Pickens District as a whole gained from expanded commerce, the town of Pickens, central to the life of the Barretts, suffered. Ford notes that villages bypassed by the railroads experienced unequal growth including "Pickens, located fifteen miles west of Greenville . . . [which] had four stores doing business in 1850 and only six stores doing business a decade later."[4]

The religious composition of Pickens District at that time is evident from its churches. The 1860 census identifies one Lutheran church (reflecting the German community in Walhalla), two Union churches, six Presbyterian churches, fifteen Methodist churches, and twenty-four Baptist churches. Revealing the distribution of wealth, the six Presbyterian churches had property valued at $9,000, compared with a total valuation of $5,715 for all twenty-four Baptist churches.

Literacy levels were comparatively low. We have found no complete analysis of literacy in South Carolina during this period, but our own research and studies of the Confederate soldier suggest significant illiteracy, most marked by the use of *X* in signing documents. The 1840 census for Pickens District disclosed that there were 11,548 whites in Pickens, of whom 7,421 were under twenty years old. Of 4,127 whites who were twenty or over, 993, or 24 percent, could not read or write. David Wallace notes in his history of South Carolina that out of a total white population of 259,000 in the state in 1840, 20,000 adults were illiterate, and 70,000 between five and twenty years of age were not in school.[5] James McPherson states that at midcentury only 80 percent of the Southern white population was literate and that only one-third of the white children were enrolled in school for an average of three months per year.[6] Bell Wiley, in his classic study *The Life of Johnny Reb*, notes that 40 percent of Confederate soldiers in fourteen companies in thirteen different North Carolina regiments made marks instead of writing their names.[7]

According to the 1840 census, the Barrett household fared better than the Pickens average for adult illiteracy, with only one of six adults living in the house listed as illiterate. None of the six Barrett children, including Milton, Benjamin, and Lawrence, however, attended school in 1840. Milton and Lawrence Barrett and William A. Collett, who married Sarah Jane Barrett sometime after June 1860, could read and write, although their letters are colloquial and independent in their spelling. Benjamin Barrett appears to have been less schooled than his brothers, since his letters are markedly more difficult to decipher and reflect the effort of someone just learning to write.

It is perhaps appropriate to say a word about the letters themselves. There are thirty-three letters written by seven soldiers. (We are reasonably confident that other letters were dispersed among Barrett descendants, but we have not been able to locate more than those published.) Some of the letters, particularly the early ones, were written on good stationery, complete with Confederate verse and patriotic emblems and pictures. Later letters were written on a wide variety of materials. Milton Barrett, in a letter dated October 14, 1861, says that Lawrence had reported that he was out of paper and could not get any more.

The difficulty of obtaining stationery parallels observations by Bell Wiley in *The Life of Johnny Reb*. He notes that the elaborate stationery used by the first volunteers in 1861 quickly disappeared. Stationery of any kind became harder and harder to find. By the spring of 1863 scraps of wrapping paper were used as stationery, penciled letters received from relatives or friends were erased and the paper reused, and family members were asked to leave a blank space at the end of letters for soldiers' use. After a Confederate victory, it was not uncommon for relatives and friends of Confederate soldiers to receive letters written on Union army stationery.

Pens, ink, and envelopes also were scarce after the first year of the war. Soldiers invented their own writing implements and envelopes as well as their own stationery. Pens were made of goose and cane quills and corn stalks. Ink was made from pokeberries and oak balls. The prewar custom of sending letters folded and sealed with wax gave way to the use of envelopes at the beginning of the war, as wax was impractical and envelopes offered more privacy. As time went on and envelopes became scarce, however, soldiers resorted to making envelopes out of newspaper or reusing envelopes sent by relatives and friends.

The Confederate Postal Department was undependable and often late. Soldiers often relied on comrades going home on furlough as a safer and cheaper way of sending letters home. Camp visitors—relatives, clergymen, politicians, and servants—also frequently transported mail.

Elegant letters written by well-educated men were rare in the ranks of the Confederate army. Most letters written home were at best uneven in language used, spelling, and organization. The poor handwriting, bad spelling, random capitalization and punctuation, as well as the style, that we see in the letters in this collection were apparently typical of the Confederate private.

The letters also followed standard epistolary conventions. The typical first sentence, "It is with pleasure that I take my pen in hand to inform you that I am well, hoping these lines may reach you in due time and find you enjoying the same blessing," was apparently characteristic of the ordinary Confederate letter writer. Most of the letters in this volume follow a standard format for beginning and concluding a letter.

The letters are in large measure presented in the form in

which they were written. Spelling and capitalization are unchanged. The only concession made to reading ease has been to divide the occasionally unbroken flow of words into sentences and paragraphs. Some letters were so organized, but the majority were not. We show the letters as they are, not only for historical accuracy but also to convey the patterns of thought and language of these up-country Confederates.

Of the thirty-three letters presented, twenty-nine are from three brothers, Milton, Lawrence, and Benjamin Barrett, and their sister Sarah Jane's husband, William Collett. There is one letter from Jasper Strickland, an apparent admirer of Malinda Barrett, another sister; two from a neighbor, Laban Mauldin; and one from a fellow soldier of Milton's, J. B. L. Wall. Notably, these letters were written by men older than what some have regarded as the eighteen- or nineteen-year-old norm for the Confederate soldier. Milton Barrett was thirty-three or thirty-four when the war began; Benjamin was probably thirty, and Lawrence, twenty-nine. Jasper Strickland was twenty-five, and William Collett was twenty-three. Only neighbor Laban Mauldin, born in 1842, fits the stereotype.

It is also appropriate to comment on the variations in the personalities and attitudes reflected by our letter writers; indeed, part of the interest of these letters lies in the very real emotions presented by the different soldiers. Jasper Strickland is animated, descriptive, and clearly writing for the benefit of a young lady at home. Laban Mauldin, who had been a soldier for two years before we meet him, is disheartened by the war. William Collett is brief and serious. Benjamin Barrett comes across as attractively naive and comparatively gentle; our sympathy is ensured by his efforts to overcome his deficiencies in writing. Lawrence Barrett first appears as a soldier in the early stages of the war; after his conscription his letters are gloomy, and he is weighed down by his feelings of responsibility for the family farm.

Our greatest exposure, however, is to Milton. He described himself as easygoing and one who could take things as they came. His letters do bear out his statement that "we must make our self contented on what ever condision we are place in." Milton appears to have adjusted well to army life. In December 1861, after more than six months in service, he noted that he had never enjoyed better health, and later letters reflect only bouts of diarrhea. He also wrote that he had not been "crost" for missing roll call or put in the guardhouse, and it is not surprising to learn from J. B. L. Wall that Milton was "always" at his post. He was a regular correspondent, who appeared to have been anxious to maintain contact with family and friends. He does not seem particularly religious, although he attended a "babtis" church while in Goldsboro, North Carolina, in November 1861. His letters show few signs of discouragement or disillusionment, yet he was certainly susceptible to the rhetoric and florid phrases of the period, particularly during the early stages of the war.

Milton Barrett was a person of independent opinion, offering observations on the Texans with whom he fought, various officers, and events affecting the Confederacy. On March 28, 1862, Barrett described the Texas regiments, for example, as "the most disapated foot soldiers in servis," although he observed that he would "as soon fought by the side of a Texan as any for tha are brave and fought like tigers." He passes on reports and rumors and realistically states that "we hear a plenty of news but a litle that i can put confadents in." Milton Barrett emerges as a relatively

Milton Barrett, CSA

reliable reporter describing with common sense a variety of daily happenings. The letters overall convey an impression of a decent, likable man and a solid soldier.

These letters, for us at least, assumed added force with the realization that Milton, Lawrence, and Benjamin Barrett and their brother-in-law William Collett all died for the Confederate cause.

ONE

Goin to Fight
the Yankees,
1861

One might think that the inhabitants of Pickens District, which had comparatively few slaves and a preponderance of yeoman farmers, would have opposed secession, or at least would have been equivocal in their position. Residents of other areas with similar characteristics, such as east Tennessee and the more mountainous regions of Virginia and North Carolina, were at best lukewarm supporters of the Confederacy. Such does not appear to have been the case in Pickens, or indeed in any other area of South Carolina. Lacy K. Ford, Jr., has explored the attitudes in the up-country and suggests that there was near unanimity of support for the Confederacy.

By the time the secession convention was called in December 1860, most white South Carolinians appeared convinced that their way of life, based on what Ford describes as slave-labor–based republicanism, was imperiled by the election of a Republican president. In the election for delegates to the convention, for example, Unionist B. F. Perry, a power in Greenville District for decades, lost his first election ever, receiving 225 votes compared with 1,300 for secessionist candidates.[1] Although we have found no record of the vote in Pickens District, Spartanburg elected secessionists overwhelmingly, as did the other up-country districts. The November and December issues of the *South Carolina Spartan*, a weekly newspaper in Spartanburg District, demonstrated support and enthusiasm for secession during the weeks leading up to the secession convention. The newspaper publicized secessionist meetings and published updates on activity in the state legislature as well as notices to citizens encouraging them to support the Confederate cause.

At the secession convention on December 20, 1860, the Ordinance of Secession was adopted by a vote of 170 to 0. Among those voting for secession were the five delegates from Pickens District. Ford concludes that "in the final analysis, a unified South Carolina could secede because the dominant ideal in her society was not the planter ideal or the slaveholding ideal, but the old 'country-republican' ideal of personal independence, given peculiar fortification by the use of black slaves as a mud-sill class. Yeoman rose with planter to defend this ideal because it was not merely the planter's ideal, but his as well."[2]

The firing upon Fort Sumter on April 12, 1861, was publicized almost immediately in the town of Pickens (also known as Pickensville) and the other small communities in upper South Carolina. The reaction was enthusiastic support for the Southern cause. Within two days, Company I of the Fourth Regiment was organized at Pickensville, and others were to follow. By January 1862 Pickens District had sent fourteen companies to the Confederacy, and six more were ready to join.[3]

The number of soldiers from Pickens District was impressively high, particularly when compared with population figures. In 1860 Pickens had a total white population of 15,335. Although no breakdown for Pickens is available,

18.9 percent of the total white population in South Carolina as a whole consisted of white males between the ages of eighteen and forty-five. If this ratio were applied to Pickens District, there would have been roughly 2,900 white males between eighteen and forty-five. Thus, the furnishing of twenty companies — or approximately 2,000 men, based on the Confederate Congress's determination in March 1861 that each company should consist of 102 men — was an impressive response to the Confederacy's call.[4]

Among those immediately rallying to the Southern cause was William Lawrence Barrett. Lawrence enlisted on April 14, the same day that the Stars and Stripes was lowered at Fort Sumter. As we have seen, Lawrence Barrett, still a bachelor at twenty-eight, was the only adult male on the Barrett farm, but he does not appear to have hesitated in his decision to volunteer.

W. Lawrence Barrett enlisted as a private in Company I, Fourth Regiment, South Carolina Volunteers. This regiment was first organized in Anderson, South Carolina, in March 1861. Barrett, who enlisted for twelve months' volunteer service, was enrolled at Pickensville on April 14, 1861, and was initiated into Confederate service at Columbia, South Carolina, on June 7, 1861, by Barnard E. Bee, lieutenant colonel and mustering officer.[5] J. B. E. Sloan was colonel of the Fourth Regiment at this time.

The first wartime letter of this collection was sent to Jesse McMahan by Lawrence.

June the 7th, 1861

Deare Sir   I take the present opportunity to inform you that I am well at this time hoping these lines may find

Confederate soldier, probably William Lawrence Barrett

you all well. I reached Columbia safe and found all moderately well except some cases of mumps. there is nothing new in Columbia but was mustered into the Confedrate serves to day at 10 o clock. it is not none when we leave heare. write to me Soon and tel mother and all the rest that I am well and doing fine. I will write the nuse when I hear it. nothing more at Present.

W. L. BARRETT

[Reverse states, "Dress parade is over and no orders from head quarters."]

Lawrence Barrett's regiment left Columbia on June 15, 1861, reached Richmond on June 17, and by June 23 had arrived at Camp Carolina near Leesburg, Loudoun County, Virginia. Jesse W. Reid, a private from Greenville, South Carolina, in Company C, described the Fourth Regiment's trip from Columbia to Richmond some thirty years later: it "beat anything that I ever saw for non-discipline and in subordination in soldiers. It seems that every man in the regiment mistook himself for Commander-in-Chief of the regiment."[6] Reid reported that whiskey was plentiful and cheap on that journey. He referred to the times at camp near Leesburg as being the best of the war. According to him, the soldiers "lived like kings" and "had the company and the sympathy of as fine a set of ladies as lived on God's green earth."[7]

Sloan's Fourth South Carolina regiment played a significant role in the first major battle of the war, on July 21, 1861. Although Sloan's Regiment had been transferred on June 20 to the brigade of Colonel Jubal A. Early, it was subsequently assigned to a temporary brigade commanded by Colonel

Nathan George ("Shanks") Evans, consisting of the Fourth, Wheat's Louisiana Battalion, two companies of Virginia cavalry, and four six-pounder guns. Shanks Evans (1824–68), of Marion, South Carolina, was educated at Randolph Macon College and West Point. Despite early success (he was made brigadier general on October 21, 1861, after a fine performance at Ball's Bluff), Evans never achieved higher rank or reputation, in large measure because of alleged problems with alcohol.

Evans's Brigade was at the center of the first battle of Bull Run, or First Manassas. The brigade was stationed at the extreme left of the Confederate line, assigned to protect the Stone Bridge. On July 21, just as the Confederates planned to attack the Union's left, Northern commander Irvin McDowell sent two divisions to cross at Sudley's Ford, some two miles to the left of Evans at the Stone Bridge. Evans left four companies of the Fourth South Carolina to guard the Stone Bridge and took the remaining six companies of the Fourth and the rest of his brigade to counter the Federal advance. Evans's Brigade, the first to counter the Union forces, fought vigorously during the early stage of the battle.[8] Of the Fourth Regiment, eleven were killed, and seventy-nine were wounded.

While Lawrence Barrett was seeing Virginia and presumably combat for the first time, Jasper Strickland was expressing his wonderment at Charleston and the sea. Strickland, of Anderson County, apparently admired Malinda Barrett, Lawrence's younger sister, who was seventeen years old at the outbreak of the war. Aged twenty-five in 1861, Strickland enlisted in the Confederate army at Greenville, South Carolina, and was enrolled on July 1, 1861, at Summerville by Captain Spartan D. Goodlett. His enlistment, which lasted only until April 11, 1862, was in Company K (Captain S. D. Goodlett's Company), Sixth Regiment, South Carolina Volunteers.[9]

Strickland's marvelous letter was obviously written with the expectation that it would be read to or by Malinda Barrett.

Summerville, S.C.   July 14, 1861

Mr. Jesse McMahan
Dear Sir,

I take the present opportunity to write a few lines to inform you that I am well and hope they will find you injoying good health. I have injoyed my self prety well senc I have ben down hear But not like up their. I would like to see you all very well But I dont expect I will get to see you soon. We start to virginia Day after to morrow. I may never see you again But I hope I will see you all again.

I have Ben to Charleston. I saw Many things their. I saw the cannon. I Rode on the steem Boat. it was a delightful Ride. there is water melon, peaches, mush melion, Ripe hear corn in Rosin ears.

We have Ben prety well treated sence we came down But I would Rather Be At home for their is no place like home. I would like to see all the girls up thear for there is no girls down hear. what few that is is so ugly that A man hates to look. I thought it wail to keep from hurting my eyes. this is the truth cirten.

tell Linda Barrett that I would like to see her veary much. But I Recen I will not see her soon But I hope I will get to see some time Agian. tell Ann King that John Bucknell says he will never forget her and he sends his Beste

Respects to her. tell all the children howdy for me well else tell them good By for me. I am a goin to fight the Yankees and I expect to conker though I may Die But I can think I will if I live I am comain Back yet agian.

I have saw tow Aleigaters young ones. I saw some large fish in the sea. we get A long to geather pretty well. ther has not Bin any fighting in our company since we come down But some drunk fellow came in and some one whipped him. their is A Bought one thousand Solgers in camp hear. we have not yet no water to Drink down hear But warm water and mud. Let your Brothers see this letter if you pleiz. I give my Bes Respect to all. I might not write til I muster Agian. I muste cloze.

JASPER STRICKLAND

Jesse McMahond

Milton Barrett, who wrote most of the letters in this volume, enlisted in the Confederate army on June 13, 1861, at Camp McDonald in Cobb County, Georgia. He registered as a private in Company A, First Regiment, Fourth Brigade, Georgia Volunteers. Company A was known as the Acworth Rifles and was largely drawn from Acworth, Georgia, a small town in Cobb County northwest of Atlanta. The Acworth Rifles were joined by nine other companies from the central and western parts of the state. The ten companies in what was to become the Eighteenth Georgia were recruited from seven counties, with Bartow County furnishing four companies.

Milton Barrett was in training at Camp McDonald in Cobb County until August 3, 1861, when his unit left for Richmond, Virginia. He wrote his first letter to his sister and brother-in-law, Lucretia Caroline and Jesse McMahan, from Camp McDonald.

Camp Mcdonel the 4th Brigade   *August 2, 1861*
   Dear Brother and sister   hit is with pleasure i take my pen in hand to let you know that i am well hoping when thes lines comes to hand tha may find you enjoying the same blessing.

We leave hear on the 3 inst for virginia. We have bin hear ever scenc the 11th of June last a drilling. we are wel drill and armd and preparde to meat the enemy any wher. georgia has spent $10000 in drilling us be side our arms and quipments and i am shore when you hear from the forth Brigade of georgia you well hear of Some good fighting and the most marvels case is 3000 of us have bin hear all most two months and but one death in the Brigade and that was in the Daivis invincebels from Disty county [Company D, Eighteenth Georgia, organized in Dougherty County]. the health of the brigade is good. some measels and mumps.

you i know have heard of the glouris victor of Manassis. we have the victor to rejoyis over while we have many frends ther loss to moand. Of many who i was persely acquainted with but one concilation tha dide in the most glouris case cornel Bartow most lamented he fell while chargen on the batry.[10]

you must show this letter to mother an tel hear not to be uneasy about me but to be proud rather than serow that she has two sons engage in the cose of ther cuntry and if you toment a tall let hit be be cose you have not twenty engage in the glouris cose. if i fall in the batel feal or deide

Jesse and Lucretia Caroline McMahan, ca. 1886

in camps of the victors my body will be sent to you to be
buried wherever you see proper. As for my part i have no
chois wher my body is lade after hit cant serve hits cuntry
no moar but i hope we may be victorous and i may soon
return home to enjoy frends and cuntry. When you rite
to me direct your letters to the first Rigement of the forth
Brigade of georgia volingtiers compeny A.

So i must close for the drum is a beating for perade. i am
your loving Brother.

Milton Barrett

Jesse and Caroline McMahan

Death or Liberty

The Acworth Rifles were mustered into Confederate service for three years or the duration of the war at Richmond
on August 9, 1861. Once in Richmond, Milton Barrett's
unit was renamed Company A, Sixteenth Regiment, Georgia Volunteers. The regiment was initially camped near the
reservoir but then was moved to the lower part of the city
in order to guard prisoners of war.

Richmon verginia　　　　　　　　　*August 11th Day   1861*
　　Dear Brother and Sister　　　hit is with pleasure i take
my pen in hand to let you know that i am wel hoping thes
lines may find you enjoying the same blesing. hit is all ways
expected of those at home when tha git a letter from a solger in serves to hear all that is a going on in the armey but
hit is a mis stake. a sholger nows but litle moar what is a

goin on than you do only in his own ridge ment or when
he receves orders to march and than he dont know whether
hit is for a fight or to change en campements til he sees the
enmey. only by the movements of the arrney he can give a
perty close gest. i know that tha is fifty Thousand shoulgers in camp hear and sixteen Hundred yankee prisoners
hear but i dont know how long we wil stay her nor wher we
will go to next.

we left camp Mcdonle on the 3 inst and got hear on the 7
a distence of 600 miles. we had a fine time of hit. we was
cherd all a long the way by croud of sitecens. a flag was
a waven over most ever house and every winder crouded
with ladys and the sides of the road linde with them throwing appels and boquets of flowers in the cars. the best and
warmest and best fealing was shound to us all the way.

we stade 24 hours at noxville camp in James ilent then
we got orders to march. we then came to this place 200
miles. we ar well situated hear with good water and plenty
to eat and this is the best cuntry and the pretest place i
ever saw and the best corn i ever saw and the most tobacco,
clovers fields and grass pasture, fine horses and cows and
stock of all sorts.

i am anxheers to hear from Laurence. you said he was
in the forth ridge ment. hit was engage in the battle
of Manassa but i have not saw no list of the dead nor
wounded. i shal write to Manassa and i wont you to write
to me soon and give me all of the infirmation you can.
direct your letters to Richmon vergina sixteenth Ridgement of ga volingtiers Co A. our number has change seence
we have come hear. tha is some sickness in our camps to
day. we hant had but one death in our ridgement.

give my best respects to all inquireng frends and expect the same yourself.

your brother

MILTON BARRETT

J and C McMahan and Frends

By the middle of October 1861 Milton Barrett's regiment had again been renamed. The Sixteenth Regiment had been redesignated the Eighteenth Regiment and was commanded by William Tatum Wofford. Wofford (1824–84), a lawyer and newspaperman from Cassville, Georgia, served as a captain in the Mexican War. Although he voted against secession as a member of the Georgia state convention, he supported his state when war came. He was appointed a colonel on April 25, 1861. In the 1862 campaign around Richmond, Wofford and the Eighteenth Georgia fought in Hood's Texas Brigade. At Second Manassas, South Mountain, and Antietam, Wofford commanded the brigade as senior colonel. The Eighteenth Georgia then became part of T. R. R. Cobb's Brigade; when Cobb was killed at the battle of Fredericksburg in late 1862, Wofford succeeded him in command of the brigade. Wofford was promoted to brigadier general to rank from January 17, 1863, and served until the end of the war. He was a solid and dependable commander.

The captain at this time of Milton's Company A was Captain J. B. O'Neill.[11]

Camp Winder
Richmond   *Oct 14, 1861*

Dear Brother and Sister—Thrue the kind provadents of
and all wise god i am enjoying good health while many of
my Brother solgers has sicken and dide hoping thes lines
may find you all well.

i have nothing that will interrest you mutch to write. we
hear a plenty of news but a litle that i can put confadents in.
We will git a dispatch one day and the next hit will conter-
dicted. we heard some time ago that our army had crost
the potomic but hit is not so but hit will have to be cross
before the city can be taken for to march men to the tenth
highths would be foley. We will have to force them out by
sorounding them and cuting them of from ther soplise.

We are still aminding our yankees in ther cage. i beleve
i told you in my letter that we was a garden the prisnors
about 2000. We have bin a garden them one month and has
to gard them another. We have sent five 100 to new orleans
but tha git no les, tha are like the widers oil tha send in
moar or less evry weak.

i will say to you that i am a giting use to doing with thou
sleap and a giting fat on poridge. Owing to the sicness that
has bin in our regement and caren off prisnours whitch 100
of our reg has bin engage in the gard duty has bin heavy
on us we wones. Four nights sleep in a weak has bin a rear
thing with me for the last month but our reg is enproving
in health and i hop soon to see our ranks full. But thirty
of our brave boys is gon to return no moar. three from my
company who sleep in the silent room wer tha will wake no
moar. ther vakens in ranks can be fill with others but in the
sirkle of frends at home and a round fiar side tha neve can

be fild. We bered them in the oners of war and mark the place so ther friends may find ther graves.

i have not had a letter from Laurence in two weaks. He was wel and sed he was out of paper an could not git any thare. i sent him a bundle of paper an envelops by express and ask him to write whether he got hit or not but i have not got no ancer. About that time his reg was orded to march to Monson hill but tha are now back at ther olde camps. We have a rite smart the vantage of a grate many of our trops being clost to a place wher we can buy any thing that we nead. i told Laurence any thing he could not git thar to let me know an i would send hit too him by express. We are a giting a good sply of winter clothing a grate deal sent us from gorgia. We also haf a plenty of sugar and coffe. Some of the trops cannot get hit reglar on the account hit cannot be ship to them.

i have to day receive your letter and Malinda. i had jest rote and Seald one to send to Malinda when i got hern. hit saved her from giting bringer for not writing. i will send her my ambertype in a few days and ancer her letter, i will not send the one that i had rote. i was glad to hear from you all an sorrow to hear of Mary a losing her darling babes but we must make our self contented on what ever condision we are place in. In fack, i do i take everthing easy, i hear hit oftimes repeted by members of my copeny. i wish i could enjoy myself as well as hit looks like you do. i wont to see you all but i expect hit wil be some time be fore i have that pleasure. i was musterd into servest for durin the war or three year whitch four months of the time is gon.

We have to send of some moar prisnors. i expect to go with the next croud and as we have to go by colomba i am a going to try mity heard to git to come back by and see you all but i cant tel how hit will be. give my love to all enqureing frends and except the same your self. write ofin and a heap of hit.

i am your loving brother

MILTON BARRETT
Camp Winer
Richmond Va.
18 reg ga V. co A
in the cear of captain
J B O Neal

Disease, a major concern throughout the war, killed more soldiers than enemy arms. In 1861 particularly, large numbers of rural young men were exposed to a variety of illnesses for which they had little immunity. Measles, for example, broke out in Milton's regiment shortly after the Eighteenth Georgia reached Richmond. Milton notes that "thirty of our brave boys is gon to return no moar," including three from his company. In one of the few company reports for the Eighteenth Georgia in the National Archives, Captain Samuel Irvin of Company D wrote of the months before December 31, 1861. The number of soldiers on his sick list for the months of November and December averaged ten per day, or about one-sixth of the company. He said that "the worst of the cases were occasioned by exposure causing severe colds which generally yielded to treatment" and that there were several cases of mumps. Company D had six deaths during its first six months of service.

In late October 1861 Milton Barrett and the Eighteenth

Georgia were transferred from Richmond to Goldsboro, North Carolina, to counter a threatened Federal invasion of the Carolina coast. By orders dated November 5, the Eighteenth Georgia and the Second Texas were assigned to the command of General Joseph E. Johnston. On November 9 or 10 Colonel Wofford's brigade was sent back to Richmond, and then to northern Virginia. The Eighteenth Georgia infantry was soon encamped near Dumfries, Virginia.

In one of his longer letters home, Milton Barrett wrote a daily account of life in camp near Goldsboro and of his brigade's journey through North Carolina and Virginia.

Goldsboro

North Carolina   Waynes County

1861

October 28   day clear and cool with a heavy frost. our streets is crowded with sitseers some a trading an some for curiosity. they are a bringing in all kinds of produce that the cuntry a fords at mutch loar price than we could buy in richmon sweet potatoes at 40 cts a bushel chickens at 15 cts a pece and we drew fish and peas extrey of what we have bin a drawing but no coffee. for the first time we have mist the ladys like all others i have found in the southern states kind an benevlent an a doing all in ther power for ther cuntry and welfar of the shoulgers in serves.

Tuesday the 29   we have orders to keap two days rashons cook and nap sackes pack and hold our self in readness to march at a minets notis. hit is thout that a fight will commence to day at wilmaton. the new york fleat is in site an the train is a wating with the engine fiard up.

i can see a man on horse back ever hour a going from the telagraph ofis to the colnels quarters. the probilty is that we will be in a fight be fore five hour passe by.

Wednesday the 30   the weather is cool and pleasant and the health of our army in proving very fast. the fleat plade off an did not attempt to land. we had our reaglar drills an a large arsenal at dress perade. Doctor Mase of Acworth got hear to day and our company has hiard him to wait on. we was a neading a good Doctor very bad. wc do not like the one that belongs to the regement.

Thursday 31   warm and down appearance of rain. i see nor hear nothing of emportans to day. Colnel Lee actain as general enspected our troops to day and we are still helt in readiness.[12] i paid 60 cts a pound for coffee to day.

Friday November the 1   every thing seams still today. the same auld tail keep two days rashon cook. we have bicets that is so hard i could nock a bull down with one. hit is raining this eaven an the wind a blowing a prospeck of a stormey night.

Saturday 2   last night will be long remembered by many a sholger. the rain continud to fall an the wind increast. by midnight our tents was blowed down an every thing rining wet and the earth so soft and the wind a bloing we could not get our tents to stand. hit stop at day light and the sun is a shining an everthing a drying very fast. we fist up our tents an dried our close and blankets and all write again.

Sunday the 3   clear and pleasnt. nothing is heard of the yankees fleat. hit is thout that tha was lost in the storm on friday night. after our usel inspection of guns and tents i went out in town. after a few hours ramble over town i went in to a babtis church. the house was crowded with sitseers and shoulgers and many a pair of perty eyes a pipen from under a straw hat drest with ribon an artifical flowlers. goldsboro is a new settle place and a junction of four rail rods with sevrel church houses an a few fine bildings a leavel and butiful location 3000 inhabants and the buldings scatered so hit dont look weel.

Monday the forth   tha was 74 yankees brong hear today tha was capture near hatters fort on Saudrday. tha belong to the fleat that we have bin a watching. ther vesel blowed a shore loaded with horses an war equipage. the vesel and crue was all taken prisner an the rest all bload a way and are not heard of yet. on friday night while the wind was a blowing down our tens an a dreanching us hit was a fighing our battels.[13] i beleave provadents is on our side and we have nothing fear but will prove to the world that we are rite.

Tuesday the 5   cloudy and cool. noting of in portens today. ever thing seams still.

Wenday 6   nothing today. cloudy and windy.

Thursday the 7   this morning the rowl beat at 4 o'clock. we all got up an fel in lines. our orderly in form us that we had to storack tents at 6 o'clock and be ready at 12 o'clock. by 9 we had roar napsacks and haversacks pack all things ready at 12 we started traveld sloe on the account of the engine being out of order. we travel all night got to Petersburg on friday 8 layover two hour tel we could git transportation. the first train of us got to the city at five in the eaven the rest at midnight. hit seams like giting home and i beleve ever heart felt glad at the site of the old citty. our bagage has not got hear so we sleap in the barackes drew our bread ready bake and broiled our bacon on the coals drew coffee but nothing to make hit in but we faird, finley.

Saudrday 9   our bagage got hear this morning. we put up our tents and got every thing reaglated by dinner. at 2 oclock hit commenced raining and the wind a blowing and heavy thunder and very coal. hit camed off by night and we had still but coal. we have to go to manasses as soon as we trancetation. we will not stay hear but two or three days.

Sunday the tenth   hit has cleard off warm and perty day an avery buisey one with us. the in spection of guns and tents com off at ten oclock a travling an rain our guns was in a bad fire an hit took heard work to get them so tha would pass an at 2 oclock from a ginrel revew come on we all had to cary out napsacks and haversacks and canteens. we was keep in the feil thre hours then drest perrade and orders read to march to manases with thout any unnessary delay. we was all glad to hear tatto so we could go to bead.

Monday the 11   cloudy and warm. rite mart stur to day a makeen prepration to leav the good old city. hit will be a day or two be fore we can git transportation owing to the many troops a leaving hear for west vergina. i paide to day one dollar and fifty cents to git one piar of shoes half sold.

Tuesday 12   to day we moved our sick all to one hos-pitel bor up all of our cloves that we coul not toate easey. we will leave them hear. we are a maken preperation for marching a foot. i hear bad news from georgia an tenasee five rail road bridges burnt by the union men 2 in georgia and 3 in tenasee.

Wendsday 13   the weather is pleasant for the season. nothing strange in our camps a const stur a mong trops some a coming in an some a leaven for other pints. we are a staing hear under marching orders. no teling what day we wil leave.

Thrusday the 14   cloudy and raining but warm. we was to day return from under genrel lee back to the war depart met. we are Still under the orders to go to west vergina. nothing in terestin in our camp. trops has bin a leaving hear sevrils days. our time will come in a few days. we dont no what pint we will go.

Friday 15   cloudy with some rain. we are a doing noting today. the doors is all shut to day in the city no traiding a going on all a ceaping hit as a day of thanks given. i receive a leter from Laurence today staten that he was well an had receive a letter from home staten that all was well an Benjamon Barrett and James McMahan was goin on the coast an all of the rest that was able for camp life except John Archa and his paper and envelop that i sent him has got thar.

Sunday 16   winday an cold. nothing of intrust to day. i went to sevrel of the hospital today looking for Joph/King but i could not find him. i heard that he is hear sick.

Sunday the 17   clear and cold. this eaven we receve orders to cook two days rashon and be ready to start to Fedricburg by eight oclock to morow. we are all buisey a cooking the boys all in fine spirits. we haf a joley time.

Monday 18   we left richmond at 8 Am past thru Ashville. this is a smol and olde looking place. hit is the place that give birth to the grate stateman Henry Clay. we past thru a hiley and old fiels for 15 miles. the next station was the junction whre the Fredicburg and manases roads crosses. the land looks better an many good farms. Milforts Station is next.

hear we git into the grate valey of vaergina. this is the

pertis and the best land i ever saw. as far as my eyes wood let me see i could see nothing but field of corn and wheat and fine houses and long rows of nigors cabins can not see no timber hardley. fences made of brush stakes drove a bout 3 feet a part and the brush work in and a ditch on one side the wheat hids the ground the corn cut down and pilde stocks and ears all to geather. we went thrue this valey 20 miles come to Fredricburg. this is the oldes city in southern states and give birth to the grate Washington. from hear we went about 10 miles to a station stade all night some pitch ther tents some spread the blankets under some pines. we all rested very well.

Tuesday the 19   this moring we loaded our bagage wagons and took up the line of march for the first time. i never saw the boys in finer spirits than tha are this moring. Colnel Woffer put a privet on his horse an he is a take hit a foot. we past over a ruff and hiley road haulted at a 11 oclock on a hill. we can hear the yankee guns down the river. one hours rest we perseded on a nare and ruff road now an then come to smoles streams and but one log to cross on. hit would take one hour for all to cross. we stop at five oclock for the night march 10 miles slep in the woods with thout tent an hit very coald but we had wood a plenty. we faird very well.

Wenday 20   we took up the line of march again for the potomac river. got hear at two in the eaven pitch tents in the woods. hit a raining and coald but we got wood a plenty. tha is sevrel troops hear and the yankees in site. we are in a briggade commanded by general Wigfaul of Texas consist of the first and second regement of Texas 600 calvery of North Carolina and Hampton legons of SC and 18th Ga with Alabam.

Thursday 21   today i can hear canons a bout every 10 minets. hit is our men a shoting at the yankees a cross the river a bout two miles wide. we are a throwing in trenchmen tha and a planting guns. the yankees is a bilding boats to cross the river an our troops a throwing bums at them. a fight will com off hear in a few days. we are stasion 18 miles be low Manases. i can not learn what the name of this county is. we are camp one half mile from the potomac river and can see the yankees as thick as black birds on the merlon side a floating bridge to cross tha are him our batterys wont let ther large vesel pass. Some time tha will slip by with a smole vesel. tha will be something in a few day. i must close. direct your letter to Richmond Va 18 th reg ga v in cear of capt oneal. i am enjoying fine health. give my love to mother an all friends. i am your loving brother

MILTON BARRETT

To Jesse and Caroline
    Memahan

Milton's letters refer regularly to events in Pickens County. For example, he noted with sadness that his sister Mary Ann, married to John Powers, had lost "her darling babes," apparently in October 1861. Of particular interest to Milton were the decisions of relatives and neighbors to enlist. As we just saw, on November 15 Milton had learned that his brother Benjamin and James McMahan "an all of the rest that was able for camp life except John Archa" were going to the coast. This is the first evidence we have that Milton's brother Benjamin had joined the Southern army.

When he joined the Confederate army, Benjamin C. Barrett, fourth child and second son of William and Mary Barrett, was hardly the model of the impetuous young volunteer. Born in 1830 or 1831 in Pickens District, he was thirty when he volunteered. He had married Martha Ann Gibson, and by 1862 he had four sons: William, Milton, David, and Benjamin.

We do not know why Benjamin Barrett volunteered, but he certainly did not join in the first burst of enthusiasm for the Confederacy. He was enrolled at Pickensville, South Carolina, on October 24, 1861, by Lieutenant J. B. E. Sloan for "three years or the war." He joined Captain Thomas H. Boggs's company (Company E). Initially attached to Orr's Regiment (First South Carolina Rifles), Company E became part of the Fifth (Moore's) Battalion on December 10, 1861. With the addition of further companies, Moore's Battalion was designated the Second South Carolina Rifles on April 27, 1862. Pay was not munificent; Benjamin received sixty-nine dollars on July 24, 1862, for four months' service, from March 1 to June 30, 1862.

A number of neighbors joined Company E with Benjamin Barrett. Indeed, the ranks of Company E were filled almost entirely with residents of Pickens District. Among those joining were James McMahan,[14] the great-nephew of Jesse McMahan, and sons of neighbor William King.[15] As noted in Milton's letter, one who did not join Company E was John Archer, son of the Barretts' neighbor Malinda Archer. Less than a month after Milton's entry, however, on December 4, 1861, John Archer joined the First Battalion of the South Carolina cavalry.[16]

Company E was initially led by Captain Thomas Hamilton Boggs. He also joined the Confederate forces on October 24, 1861, and was elected lieutenant colonel of the Sec-

Confederate picket at Charleston, South Carolina, 1861
(Courtesy of the Library of Congress)

ond Regiment Rifles on May 12, 1862. He died, however, at home in Pickens District on July 6, 1862, of typhoid fever.

The Second Regiment was initially stationed on Sullivan's Island and remained in South Carolina throughout the winter of 1861–62. Benjamin wrote his first letter to the McMahans shortly after Milton learned that Benjamin was going to the coast.

Nov. 18, 1861

Dere Broth ann Sister

hit is with pleshure to take mi pen in han to Let yo No That i am well at this time An hope that these fue lins ma find yo all well.

i have a many a strange thing to right to you. i have Sene a many a strang thing Since i sene you. Sea is a strange looking water Cause the tide rize ann falls evry twenty four ours.

we muster ann back purty please you evry Saw. we are inn proving faste. wee can muster purt near as good as en of them. we mus a bin ask seven teen commands.

i am riting bi candle lite. i have just got in from meeting. we have it twice a week and Sunday for a Rerity. But he dont sweet us mountain boys for he is a Seceder. he preaches for the South and Prays for the South and dont mention the North any at all. I want One that will preach for us and pray for us and call Nations to the South— Some but not many. He is a well spoken man and well learnt as you generly see.—we have all kine of pepel in this regiment. you know that where they is so many men.

I want you to write how Lawrence is getting along and where he is at. write to me how to direct my leters to him and write the Same about Milton for I want to hear from them back-yard News. Write soon and let me heare the news and how you are geting a long and how all are geting a long. When you write to Milton write to him so he can Direct his leters to me—Tell him we are doing fine and well satisfied as you generaly se in any one that is a going to fight four ther Country.

i must tel you what we have to eat. we have had some bacon ann some flour and beefe [illegible] an corn meale.

James MacMahon is well [illegible] i myself is in good
health at this time. i sene William Maul din there. he is
well an lucks well. he scse that when his time is out that
he will Jine Captain Baugs comane. he sees that he owes
Clurd eight dollars. Rabbit King is well. lee Bagges is a
gotten better. wount you to Rite some as often as you
can right.

    Direct your letters to Sullivans Island, Orr's Ridgment.

                    BENJAMIN BARRETT (hand)

                    right [illegible]

    Benjamin refers to having attended "meeting," and other
letters from the Barrett soldiers refer to religious gatherings.
Milton stated, for example, that he had gone to a "babtis"
church in Goldsboro on Sunday, November 3. Religious services in the Confederate army usually consisted of preaching and, more frequently, prayer meetings. Services were
conducted by chaplains, missionaries, visiting ministers, and
occasionally by laymen.

    While Benjamin Barrett was on the coast of South
Carolina, Lawrence and Milton were both in northern
Virginia. Following the battle of First Manassas, Sloan's
Fourth Regiment, including Lawrence Barrett, encamped
near McLain's Ford. Lawrence and Milton were to remain
in camp throughout the fall and winter as the Confederates faced General George B. McClellan, who was then
principally engaged in training his rapidly increasing forces.

    Lawrence wrote one of his longer letters on November 22
from Centerville.

Confederate barracks at Centerville, Virginia, March 1862
(Courtesy of the Library of Congress)

Virginia Fairefax Co Centerville Camp
first Corps of the army of the potomac
in the Confederate States of America

Nov 22, 1861

Deare Brother & sister   I availe my self of the present
opportunity of droping you a few lines to let you know how
I am geting a long. I hav not ben able to do servis for three
weeks untill now. I hav had a bad cold and you know it all

ways sarnes me at home and its worse here. I am now well
and enjoying my self as well as could be expected under the
present circumstances & in hope these lines may reach you
in due time and find you all well.

I have no news of any interest to wright. We are still
lying in weight for the approach of the enemy. We cannot
tell what day they may come on us. we are well prepared
to entertaine them and use them in the most hostile manner. this place is well fortified. there is 8 round forts for the
artilery and a line of breast works from one to the other
so they can pass with out being exposed to the enemy in
case they should want reinforcement. if this place ever is
attacked while the fort is here I am of the opinion that they
will be whiped so bad they will hardley any one go back
to tel the tale. if we cannot whip three hundred thousand
here a easier than we did one hundred at bull run I am
badly mistaken in my mind a bout it not with standing we
will be liable to loose a heap of lives. You know they never
was a large victory won with it. there has been heavy fireing in direction Evansport the few last days. I supose it is
our blockade fire on Yankeys vessels trying to run there
blockade. I hav not heard the particulars of the affare.

The weather has bin very cold and windy for some time
untill to day it is pleasant as spring and every thing only the
usual nois in camps of drums and other instruments of war.
the artilermen practisen shooting ther canons. our pickets
has ben very succesful of late as in capturen yankees. they
taken five wagons and teams and thirty two yankeys last
saturday and eleven on monday and in fact some everyday.
we are still in tents and I do not of any other arrangement.
the yankes has not goin in to [illegible] winter quarters yet

and stil thereaten to march on us but I note one thing they
are very slo a bout it. you know that a burned child dreads
the fire. it is thought by some of the carolinans that we will
not take winter quarters here at all but go back south. that
move would be agreeable to my mind and health. the wind
blows two mutch like poring cold water down a fellows
back to suit me. All of the boys is in tolerable good health.
I have not heard from Jo King in two weeks. he was then a
bout as he had been for a long time. I am surprised at him
for not goin home. he will not be fit for serves.

Yours of the 31 came in due time. the contents afforded
me a great deale of pleasure. I hav delayed in righting until
now on the account of the expected attack at this place
whitch has not come off yet. Milton has got back to richmond. he was well up to 15th inst. I want you to wright to
me as soon as posible and tel me all about the times. I heare
so many diferent tales from that part. I want to know who
all went in Boggsis Co. I heare of some that volinteered
and did not go. tel me all a bout it and the price of produce and grocers. I heare a heap of diferent tails. trashey
fruits are very high aples 40 cts Do chestnuts linders 25 cts
per qt butter 40 cts per lbs and every thing else in propor-
tion. Mother has quit wrighting to me all together. I sented
hom money to her in the care of R. E. Holcombe. I would
like to know whether she has got it or not. this brigade is
composed south carolinans Sloans 4 Jenkins 5 Winder 6
Blanden 9. general Jones comands this brigade Beauregarde
Division.

I saw general Beauregard yestaday.[17] he was round a
viewing the fortifications. I have seen prettier men than
beauregard in south carolina all tho he is a smart keen

looking man. nothing more at present and give my best respts to all enquiring friends and except the same.

W. L. BARRETT

Jesse McMahand
Caroline McMahand
and the little ones

Milton Barrett, at Dumfries, was not far from his brother Lawrence. On November 20 the Eighteenth Georgia was assigned to the Texas Brigade, which consisted of the First Texas, led by Alexis Rainey; the Fourth Texas, commanded by John Bell Hood; the Fifth Texas, led by James J. Archer; and the Eighteenth Georgia, often called the "Third Texas." The brigade was commanded by Brigadier General Louis T. Wigfall. Wigfall (1816–74) was one of the most colorful characters of the Confederacy. He was born in Edgefield County, South Carolina, and graduated from South Carolina College, but he moved to Texas in 1848. A fiery secessionist, he became a United States senator in 1859. He was an aide at the firing on Fort Sumter and joined the First Texas as colonel on August 28, 1861. He was made a brigadier general on October 21, 1861. General Wigfall resigned his commission on February 20, 1862, to become a Confederate senator from Texas. He bitterly opposed Jefferson Davis's conduct of the war.

Wigfall and the Texas Brigade spent the winter of 1861–62 near Dumfries, Virginia, protecting that sector from enemy raids. Captain Elijah Starr of Company E of the Eighteenth Georgia reported in regiment records now at the National Archives that his company had arrived at Dumfries on November 20 and by the end of the year had built a num-

ber of "comfortable cabins." Three days before Christmas
1861, Milton Barrett wrote to the McMahans from Dumfries.

Camp near Dumpfries on the Potomac
Vergina Prince William County   *Dec. 22 Day 1861*
Dear Brother and Sister   hit is with pleasure i seit my
self to in form you that i am wel hoping thes lincs may find
you all enjoying the same like blessing. we have all bin very
bissey scence we have bin hear at work a bilding batterys
and throwing up intrenchments and bilding cabbins to
winter in. we have had some crumish with the yankees but
we have not had a man hurt yet. tha have throwd bums at
us sevrel times and burst them a mong our pickets. pices
even go be tween ther feet and not hurt them. on wenday
last the yankees tride to pass our batterys. we sunk one of
ther vesels. the chains have disable a nother so tha had to
leave hit and we got hit on last tuesday. tha was a considerable fight a bove hear some 8 or 10 miles. i have not heard
the perticlars of hit. tha was five hundred yankees kild and
missing, the lost not so large on our side. our men whip the
fight. i was in hearing of the fight. The 17 and 18 messipa
regements and one Va regement was engage in the fight. i
hear that tha are cut up perty sevear. tha has bin recenly a
fight at leesburg tha drove the yankees back but i dont no
the perticlars of the fight.[18] we have been daley expecten a
fight hear and has sevrel alarms by the yankees a trying to
cross the river but the nois of our guns scears them back.
     scence i commence writen a heavy faring has commence
at our battery. i have a bout twenty rounds in a bout fifteen
minete. hit is moar vesels a trying to run our blockade. we

have the river blockaded and hit pesters them to git suplise. we are in genrel Wigfall's brigade and under the command of gen Johnson. we are wel fortifide hear and has got men a nuf to whip as many yankees as can land hear tho tha are a numbers host of them in site on the other side of the river. we can See them up in a baloone a looking at us.[19]

we are very well situate hear and could fair very well if hit was not for the picket duty we have to do. we have a plenty to eat. our meet is mostley beef and the worst is sault to season hit. we git flour and corn a plenty. tha is thousand of wheat stack up and not thrash. we press hit and takes cear of hit and we have press a mill in serves to grind hit and genrel Wigfall has press a good many hogs but hant kild yet. what i mean by pressing in servis is to go and take what we want and put our own price on hit or governmnet price on hit. this is a grate advantag to the farmers hear for tha have had to move ther famleys a way from hear and ther truck is liable to fall in the hands of the enemy if we was to git whip. they ar glad when we take ther truck.

After a cold and bad spel of weather we have had a few days of perty weather but today is very cold and looks like snow. i dont expect that tha will be mutch moar fighting tel spring for hear the winter is so bad that hit is all most imposable to travel. tha is not mutch sickness in our regement now. tha has bin three death scence we have bin hear. Doctor Mason is dead. we had him hiard to tend on our compeny and mutch regrets his death. he leaves a young wife that he maired a few months before he left Acworth, Ga. and many frends to morne his death.

i have not heard from Laurence scence i wrote. we are about fifteen miles a part but not mutch chance to viset but i think i shall go up thar in a few days if i find he is at the same place. i can get a furlow for three days. i like to hear from Benjamin and James how tha are a maken out and how tha like a sholgers life.

i never enjoyed bitter health in my life and ar heavery than i ever was and has not bin sick a day scence i have in service nor crost for not being at role call nor put in the garde house. i have got on as smoove as ever you saw but i want to be at home mity bad at Crismus to see all of my frends.

i receive your letter in due time. the contents give me mutch pleasure to hear from you and that you was all well and dont for git to write. direct your letters to Dumpfres. tel me all of the news. give my best respecks to all inquirends and except the same your self and excuse my long letter and tel Mother howdy for me and i would like to haf some of her Crismus dinner. i will close by wishing you all a hapy new year. i am your loving brother

MILTON BARRETT

Jesse and Caroline
    McMahon

Milton Barrett did not, of course, spend Christmas at home that year. Historian Richard M. McMurry describes Christmas at Dumfries as being "celebrated in such a manner that 'the next day headaches were both epidemic and contagious.'" [20]

TWO

The Dead Was
A Lying Thick,
1862

Sometime after June 1860, William A. Collett married Sarah Jane Barrett, who was born in 1841. Collett was born in 1838 or 1839, probably in Greenville County, South Carolina.[1] He was a farmer and lived, at the time of the census of 1860, in the Sterling Grove area of Greenville County.

W. A. Collett, apparently known as Tom, enlisted on December 10, 1861, as a private in Company K of the Sixteenth South Carolina Regiment.[2] The Sixteenth Regiment was raised in Greenville County in the late fall of 1861. The leader in organizing the ten companies was C. J. Elford (1820–67), a lawyer, a close friend of Unionist B. F. Perry, and the mayor of Greenville in 1860–61. The regiment was mustered into state service on December 12, 1861, with Elford as colonel and James C. McCullough (1824–92) as lieutenant colonel.[3] Its original strength was 713 men.[4]

The Sixteenth South Carolina was posted at Charleston from December 13, 1861, until February 1, 1862.

Campmore
Charleston, South Carolina
January 16th 1862
My Dear Brotherilawe
    i seat my Self down to in form you that i am Well hoping

the few lines may find you Well and staying Well. i have nothing Strange to Rite you only that We have A heap of sickness in Camps of Measels and Mumps. We are statian in the surburbs of Charleston. We don't now When we will move from her. tha speak of moveing us to Addams Run A Bout thirty miles from Charleston. i don't think that there is Eny chance for A fite her at tall my Self. i want you to Rite how your youngist son is A giting A long and if you don't think my Docter cant beat him. i want you to give me all the news off the country. give my best Respects to all in qiren frends. tell Jane that i think that she hirts her Self A Riting to me. I must come to A close for this time. your affecnet Brotherinlaw until Death.

WILLIAM A. COLLETT

Jesey Macmahon
Arnels Mills P.O.
Pickens District, S.C.

The report that the Sixteenth Regiment was to move to Adams Run proved correct. The regiment left Charleston on February 1, 1862; it was to remain at Adams Run until May 6, 1863, as one of the units defending the coast of South Carolina. Actual and threatened incursions by the Federal army in South Carolina required significant numbers of Confederate troops. When General Beaurgard assumed command of Southern forces in South Carolina on September 24, 1862, his command included 202 companies of all arms and 12,544 officers and soldiers.[5]

Collett's Regiment was reorganized on April 28, 1862. It was transferred from state to Confederate service for three years or the duration of the war. Elford was replaced as colonel of the Sixteenth by Lieutenant Colonel James C. McCullough.

The Sixteenth Regiment for much of 1862 and early 1863 was included in the Second Military District, under the command of Brigadier General Johnson Hagood. Hagood (1829–98) was from Barnwell, South Carolina, and graduated from the South Carolina Military Academy in 1847. A lawyer when the war came, he was elected colonel of the First South Carolina Volunteers and fought at First Manassas. He was promoted to brigadier general on July 21, 1862. He participated in South Carolina coastal defense until May 1864; thereafter he fought in Virginia and North Carolina and surrendered with General Joseph E. Johnston. Following the war, Hagood took an active part in the restoration of home rule and was elected governor of South Carolina in 1880.

While at Adams Run, the Sixteenth participated in few military engagements. It was ordered to Wilmington, North Carolina, to counter a threatened Federal landing and was stationed in that city from December 17, 1862, until early January 1863. Otherwise it remained at Adams Run. It was from Adams Run that Collett took furlough in the late summer of 1862, from August 29 to September 9.

Milton Barrett fought with Hood's Texas Brigade throughout the great battles of 1862. Brigadier General Louis T. Wigfall resigned from the army, and thus from his command of the brigade, on February 20, 1862, to assume a seat as a Texas senator in the Confederate Congress. Colonel James J. Archer of the Fifth Texas temporarily took command, but only until March 12, when John Bell Hood was promoted to brigadier general in charge of the brigade.

John Bell Hood (1831–79) represents to some both the

strength and weakness of the Confederacy as a fighting force. Born in Kentucky in 1831, Hood graduated near the bottom of his class at West Point in 1853. An outstanding subordinate commander, Hood was both aggressive and courageous and led his units with distinction in 1862 and 1863. He was badly wounded in the arm at Gettysburg and lost a leg at Chickamauga. Promoted to lieutenant general on February 1, 1864, and full general in July 1864, he led the Army of Tennessee to disaster in Tennessee in late 1864. At both Franklin (November 30) and Nashville (December 15–16), the South suffered catastrophic defeats.

Regardless of later problems, Hood and his brigade earned long-lasting fame for their performance during 1862. On March 8 the Eighteenth Georgia, along with the rest of Hood's Brigade, broke camp at Dumfries and began to march south. The warmer weather of early March thawed the ground, making the move difficult. After four days of marching, the brigade arrived at its new campsite two miles west of Fredericksburg, Virginia, along the Rappahannock and Rapidan rivers. The brigade remained in camp for most of the month, resting and training.

Fredericksburg vergina March the 28th Day 1862
Dear Brother and Sister   it is with pleasure that i take my pen in hand to let you know that i am wel hoping when thes few lines comes to hand tha may find you all enjoying the same like blessing. i receive yours of the 7 inst. its contents give me mutch pleasure to hear from you all and tha you all was well. i have nothing new to write. we have had a few pleasnt day puts me in mind that pleasnt spring is approaching with all off her butys but every thing hear has

Confederate fortifications at Manassas, Virginia, March 1862
(Courtesy of the Library of Congress)

the appearence of Jenuary not a bud to be seen on the hills
nor a flower to adorne the buty of the gardens an valeys nor
the sweet notes of a bird to cheer the wearied soldier as he
faithful stands at his post. no odd how sever the storm nor
hot the sun his duity must be don for he owes it to his self
his friends and cuntry.

we are some better situated than we was when i wrote
last. we have got something to cook in an some straw in
our tents an draws full rashons but we again have marching
orders but i dont no wher it may be to meet the yankees.
i hear tha ar advancen in large forces. we have a large
force hear but i dont be leve that Johnson aims to make a
stand hear for we ar not a fortifying hear. i think he aims
to fall back when tha gits hear and tha big battle will be
fough near Richmond. Richmond is wel fortify and tha
ar a mountain moar guns thar. it is imposable for them to
every march a army thar that will be able to take richmond.
we will soon have a fleat of sixty steamers compleated on
james rivor and forty at Fedricksburg. tha is fifteen hundred men at work at them hear. our troops have bin whip
in Tenssee and cut to peaces. the union men in tenssee is
worst than the yankees and we are a going to have troble to
get rid of them. our troops is in bad condishion for marching. the exporsure and fatig we have had scince we have
left our winter quarters has cose a grate deal of sickness a
mong soldiers and a grate many recruits have jest come and
the most of them is sick.

i have not *got no letters from Laurence in two month*. i have
wrote to him sevrels times but got no ancer. i suppose he
has not bin able to write. Benjamin has not wrote. i have
not had the chance to see any thing hear for we are not a
lowd to go out of camps and *tha is gard posted at every privet*

house to *keep the soldiers from pesture ther propery* and we
have had to drill four hour a day and be sides sevrel revews.

i am mutch *better pleas with gen Hood than i was at firs* but
the Texas regements is the most disapated foot soldiers in
servis and it takes the tites dissipland to keep them rite and
we are in a texans brigade and when we are in rome we
have to do like rome. i had as soon fought by the side of
a Texan as any for tha ar brave and fought like tigers but
tha are like a spiret horse. tha are hard to mandage and
we have to submit to ther reins. not that i hav any envey
a ginst thes brave men makes me wont to get out of this
brigade but be case i dont like to be governerd by the same
dissipland tha have to be.

give my best respects to all enquiren frends an except the
same your self and write soon. i will close by signing   your
effecnate brother
To Jesse and Caroline   MILTON BARRETT
Mcmahan

PS March the 31 day 1862

as i have delade mailing this letter i will ad a few moar
lines. it has bin a snowing and sleeting and a raining scence
i wrote the first. we are a gain a fealing the chil of the winter storms and helt in marching order pack ready to start
at a minets notis and onley a waiten for the right wing of
the Potomac to get out of danger then we leve. it may be to
day. we are a going to fall back. our pickets has had some
crumishing and has taken some prisons and four of the
Texas rangers has bin taken prisnors.
                                        M BARRETT

On April 6 Hood's Brigade received orders to be ready
to march from Fredericksburg within an hour's notice. The
Eighteenth Georgia left on April 8, and by the tenth the
entire brigade was en route to Yorktown to join General
Johnston and the other Confederate forces. When Hood's
Brigade reached Milford Station on the tenth, it boarded a
train for Ashland Station, about fifteen miles north of Richmond, arriving on the morning of April 11. The brigade
remained at Ashland Station for a few days, resting, drilling,
and cleaning equipment.

Ashland vergina   *April 11th 1862*
Dear Brother and sister   it is with pleasure that i take
my pen in hand to let you know that i am wel hoping thes
fue lines may find you enjoying the same like blessing. The
marches and counter marches we have had scence i wrote
last has been newmers.

on the night of the third at midnight we receive orders
that the enemy was advancing on us in large forces was
then in ten miles of us. our brigade was soon on the march
to meet the yankees by daylight. we was in three miles of
them. our advance gard come up on them. tha fled in dis-
order leven napsack blankets havor sacks cuting the horses
loos from ther wagons and fled back to ther hiden places.
our tropps capture ther plunder. we scouted a bout thru
the hills three days and return back to our camps on the
night of the 7.

It a snowing on the morning of the eight long be for
day. the role beat we was up and on march by six. the snow
had turn in to heavy rain. *it continued to rain all day*. ten
thousand of us on march the mud and water nea deep in a

heap of places and small stream to wade (at night we camp
in the woods it still araining. we sleep a little in the mud
and water the rain still a falling). on the 9 we continerd
our march. late in the even it commence snowing and a
rather terble night past off. on the morning of the tenth
the sun shind out for the first time scence we have bin on
our march. at twelve we got to milfort stasion took the
train at 3 p.m. we got to this place this morning after a
warm breakfast of coffe and biskets and bacon and a good
night rest.

i feal mutch refresh after puting my gun in order. i seted
my self on the ground with my close and blankets spred
around me in the sunshine. thout i would droup a few lines
to let you know my wher a bouts. we are with in 15 miles of
richmond. the object is to reforce our troops at yorktown
wher tha have bin engage for sevrel days. our troops have
repuls them back sevrel times the yankees or reinforces.
i dont know wherther we will be a needed at yorktown
or not.

i recond you have heard of the glorious vicktor in
Tenasee and Missipia.[6] i can not tel how long we will stay
hear but not long. we have no tents hear. i got all of my
paper wet and mudy. you can see by this sheet and it is
badly rote owing to the sir comstances. i have to write set-
ing flat on the ground a riten on my knea and the boys
jabring all a round. i have had to ancer them fifty question
scence i commence.

direct you letters to Richmond and i will be shore to get
them. i dont expect we will not be located long at a place
any moar til cold weather. let me know if you know any
thing a bout Laurence. i have not heard from him in two
months onley by your letters. i have wrote and wrote and

hav not hear from him scence i commence writen. i hear good new by good a thourity. our troops has sunk 15 vesels at the mouth of James revor (Buragarde has capture and routed the hole western army).

give my respects to all and write soon. i will close. hit may be a day or two be fore i can send this letter off. you shal hear from me soon.

i am your loving Brother

MILTON BARRETT

to Jesse and Caroline
McMahon

While Milton was in Ashland, Benjamin Barrett was stationed with the Second Regiment, Rifles, in South Carolina.

S.C. Colleton District Camp Price April, 1862

Mi dear Sister

I take Mi Pen in han to Let you No that I Am Well at this time Hoping that when the fue Lines Cum to han and find you in joing good helth, i re Sive your Letter an was glad to hear from you that you was Well. I have a Right smart of nuse to right you.

We have had a littel fite With the Yankes Pickets. Moore's Battalion was left in re zerve to mind the ferry to keap the Yankees from cutt in and Hol Kum Leagins from been Cutt off. the Yankees was fore mils from our camp. When we went too we had to li stil tha night we had no fier to warme an we like to froze. Hit was cold that night we dassin to have enne fier. Take noties that the yankees had run the gun boats up to the ferry wher we was station.

friday eavin we started to the ferry. The river was A Bout
A hundred yard A Cross but we had flats tide to gether and
walked A Cross on them. the yankees was on Edisto Island
(too edsto Islands, littel edsto and Big edsto). our men went
on littel edsto island. tha is whear tha fight the yankees.
Som went one corse and the uther went the other corse.
Nosegy island was ajoin Edisto Island.

Jest at day lite we open fier on the yankees. the yankees
Shot the Most but tha onely wounded two [illegible] agins
all the men that we had hurt we kild six and wounded too
of them and taken ninteen of them prisoners. tha march
them right up the river where Moore's Battalion was station and tha was good lucking men. tha had Buetiful youni-
forme. tha was one littel Boy (his age was Sixteen years
old) A Mong them he cride [illegible] for a time be cas he
was a litel boy. the rest luk like tha din car for hit.

Sixe of our men was sent to the Bridge where the Yankee
was Stand in gard. the yankee halt them an as sune as the
Yankee haltet them our men fired and shot him thru the
heart. sum of them shot him thru the han and leg and in
the Boddey and shot him selver plase Six shot at the time at
the Yankee as the yankee halted them. tha berded him on
Nosegy Island at the summer house on Nosegy Island. our
sogers bured him. Rap him up in A Blanket. he had a nice
par of glass tha spread them on his fase.

We tuck the Yankees to Charleston. tuck them to Columbia. we dont no where tha are now. I will change the
sub jeck Bout the Yankees. Moore's Battalion is in bad
health at this time with the feavor. some with the rhu-
matick pains. all sorts of dis eases. James Mahon is well at
this time. i think that we wil leave hear in a month at the
least. James Mahon went with us to fite the yankees. Right

sune and Tel me al of the Nuse that tha is. Noth mor at pres only re mans your fecknit Brother on tel Death

BENJAMIN BARRETT

(hand right in a hurry)

Benjamin's description of the incident at Edisto Island should be compared with a historical account. A Confederate military history account describes the event as follows:

> The force on Edisto was advanced to the northern part of the island, with a strong guard on Little Edisto, which touches the mainland and is cut off from the large island by Watts' cut and a creek running across its northern neck. Communication with the large island from Little Edisto is by a bridge and causeway, about the middle of the Creek's course.
>
> This being the situation, General Evans, commanding the Third district, with headquarters at Adams' run, determined to capture the guard on Little Edisto and make an armed reconnoissance on the main island. The project was intrusted to Col. P. F. Stevens, commanding the Holcombe legion, and was quite successfully executed. On the morning of March 29th, before day, Colonel Stevens, with his legion, Nelson's battalion, and a company of cavalry, attacked and dispersed the picket at Watts cut, crossed and landed on the main island west of the bridge, which communicated with Little Edisto. Moving south into the island, he detached Maj. F. G. Palmer, with seven companies, 260 men, to attack the picket at the bridge, cross over to Little Edisto, burn the bridge behind him, and capture the force thus cut off on Little Edisto, which was believed to be at least two companies. Palmer carried the bridge by a charge, and crossing over, left two of his staff, Rev. John D. McCullough, chaplain of the legion, and Mr. Irwin, with Lieutenant Bishop's company of the legion, to burn the bridge, and pushed on after

the retreating force. Day had broken, but a heavy fog obscured every object, and the attack on the Federals was made at great disadvantage. Palmer captured a lieutenant and 20 men and non-commissioned officers, the remainder of the force escaping in the fog. Colonel Stevens marched within sound of the long roll beating in the camps in the interior, and taking a few prisoners, returned to the mainland by Watts' cut, and Palmer crossed his command and prisoners over at the north end of Little Edisto in a small boat, which could only carry five men at a time, flats which were on the way to him having failed to arrive. Several of the Federal soldiers were killed and wounded in this affair, the Confederates having two slightly wounded. But for the dense fog the entire force on Little Edisto would have been captured.[7]

The Second Regiment, Rifles, was ordered from Adams Run, South Carolina, on May 26, 1862, and arrived on May 30 in Richmond, where General Johnston was trying to defend the capital against the forces of General McClellan. It did not participate in the battle of Seven Pines, although it was ordered to the field in support. The regiment was briefly part of the brigade of Brigadier General Roswell Sabine Ripley, and then on June 18, 1862, it became part of Brigadier General Richard Heron Anderson's brigade, which several weeks before had become part of a new division for Major General Ambrose Powell Hill. It joined just in time for the battle known as the Seven Days.

The Second Regiment, Rifles, left camp on June 26, crossed the Chickahominy River, and was engaged in battle on June 27 at Boatswain Swamp near Gaines' Mill. Six men were killed, and twenty were wounded. (It was also at Gaines' Mill that Benjamin's brother Milton and the Texas Brigade stormed Turkey Hill.) After marching back across the Chickahominy on Sunday, June 29, the unit set

Engraving of the Frayser farm, where Benjamin Barrett's
regiment was engaged in fighting on June 30, 1862. From
Century Magazine 30 (July 1885): 473. Based on a photograph
by E. S. Anderson.

up camp. The Second Regiment, Rifles, remained in camp
only twenty-five minutes, however, and then marched sixteen miles down Darby Town Road in time to participate in
battle at Frayser's Farm on June 30. Anderson's Brigade was
in the lead, and the Second Regiment, Rifles, soon suffered
casualties: 30 were killed, and 130 wounded.

Captain Thomas Boggs of Company E reported that his
unit was engaged at Gaines' Mill and had four men wounded

and was engaged again on Monday, June 30, with ten men wounded, some mortally. Among those wounded on either June 27 or (probably) June 30 was Benjamin Barrett. Wounded in the left leg, he was admitted to Chimborazo Hospital No. 1 in Richmond on June 30.

Built on a hill near Richmond, Chimborazo, the largest wartime hospital in the Confederacy, had a capacity of more than eight thousand patients. During the war, 76,000 soldiers were treated at Chimborazo. The hospital complex consisted of 150 wards, a bakery that produced 10,000 loaves of bread each day, a brewery with a daily production capacity of 400 kegs of beer, a soap factory, five icehouses, agricultural fields, and much livestock.

Even the best-stocked hospitals, however, were usually merely facilities for the spread of disease. Although hospital practices and nursing care gradually improved over the course of the war (hospitals stopped reusing bandages, for example), "surgical fevers" were endemic. Blood poisoning, gangrene, and osteomyelitis were among the most common hospital illnesses.[8]

Benjamin Barrett's leg was amputated at Chimborazo Hospital, and shortly thereafter he contracted blood poisoning. Over 97 percent of those patients who suffered from blood poisoning during the war eventually died as a result. Benjamin Barrett was no exception. He died on August 2, 1862, at Chimborazo. His widow, Martha Ann, received $61.36 from the Confederacy, representing $50.00 bounty and $11.36 for service from July 24 to August 1, 1862.

Milton Barrett and the Texas Brigade left Ashland on April 14 and marched to Yorktown, arriving April 19. The brigade

Chimborazo Hospital, Richmond, Virginia, April 1865
(Courtesy of the Library of Congress)

remained in reserve at Yorktown until early May, with little military activity. On May 3 the troops began to march to Richmond, but Hood's Brigade, as the army's rear guard, did not leave camp until after sunrise on May 4. That night the brigade camped a few miles north of Williamsburg.

On Wednesday, May 7, Hood's Brigade was the main force, supported by Colonel Wade Hampton's brigade, in the engagement at Eltham's Landing. Milton Barrett and the Eighteenth Georgia were in the rear, supporting a battery of artillery. The Eighteenth Georgia participated in the capture of approximately forty Union prisoners and eighty-four weapons. Barrett describes this action in his letter dated May 13.

Over the next few days, Hood's Brigade slowly retreated to Richmond. On May 13 the troops crossed the Chickahominy River and spent the next several weeks encamped a few miles northeast of the Confederate capital.

Kent County vergina   *May the 13th 1862*
Dear Brother and sister   hit is with pleasure that i take my pen in hand to let you know that i am well at present hoping these few lines may find you all injoying the like blesing. i have jest received yours dated May the 1 and was glad to hear from you.

i was at york town when i wrote last. scence then we have bin a marching a litle and a fighting a litle. we helt our fortification til the fourth of May having everything move to our rear. we vacated the place leaving nothing behind. our brigade was the last to leave. we layed in a line of battle two days and nights. hit taken that long for all the troops to get off. at 9 oclock on Sunday moring we took up the line

of march covring the retreat. we had not got many miles
tel we found that a bout 600 yankee calvery was in per suit
of us. we form a line of batle and our calvery soon repulce
them back with thout any loss. by two oclock we got to
williamsburg all right learning that the yankees was a going
in full speed up the river aiming to out flank us at west
point. our brigade was put in front and hured to that place.

a grate many troops was stop a round Williamsburg.
late on Sunday even the yankees advance on them and a
concidrable fight took place. hit lasted but few minits and
sevrel fell on boath sides. i am not able to give the number
but our troops drove them back and capturd ther artilery.

we march nearly all night. one divishion stop at williamsburg. the rest move on towds west point. us in front landed
with in six miles of that place by monday night.

the Yankees made a heavy actact on williamsburg at 11
on monday. tha was 3000 ingage on boath sides. the fight
lasted tel 6 in the even. the yankees reinforce all the time
and no reinforce got to our toops tel five in the even. our
troops won the fight. drove the yankees back with grate
slaughter. took 15 peces of artilary 1200 prisoners the loss
was heavy on boath sides. we had 590 kild and a large number wonded. the loss of the enemys was three times as large
as ours. i am not able to give the corect account of the kild
and wounded as i have not saw the genreals report of the
fight. perhaps you have saw a correct account by now. hit
was a hard and bloody battle.

we scouted a round untell on the night of the sixth we
learnt from our picets that a large number of Yankees had
landed near West Point earley on the moring of the 7. we
march a few miles towards the rivor. gen Hood and staff
was in front a looking wher to form his line of battle. a

yankee picket fiard at him but mist him. the yankee was
shot down on the spot. two company of the forth Texas
was deploed as cromishers and was a throwing the yankees
about right. the 18th georgia was place in rear of the artilry
to defend hit. the other three Texas reg. advance thrue a
strip o wood and was soon ingage with doble ther number.
the first Texas commanded by Col. Rainy fought like wile
cat and deserves grate honor. the fourth and fifth Texas
fought bravley. the 18th ga did not get to fiar a gun but
took some prisnors. the first Texas had 12 kild, 19 wounded,
the fourth two wonded and the fifth 5 kild 8 wounded. me
and 15 in our compeny was place out in a strip of woods to
keep the sharp shooters off. the ball fell a round us and the
bums burst among us but we escape unhurt. tha was 1200
yankees kild wounded and taken prisnors by our brigade.
Col Hamton took 200 prisnors and kild sevrel. we are ex-
pecting nother fight soon. we have fell back out the reach
of the gun boats on the chickhomey rivor.

i remain your effecnate brother tel death

MILTON BARRETT

To J. and C. McMahan

On May 22 Hood's Brigade was ordered to cross the
Chickahominy River to Meadow Bridge. Subsequently, in
the battle of Seven Pines, on May 31 and June 1, the brigade
saw very little action. Held in reserve, Hood's men stood in
a swamp in waist-deep water for a good part of May 31. By
the time they received orders to move to Nine Mile Road,
the fighting was over. Hood's Brigade was also on reserve on
June 1. Soon after the battle the brigade was back at camp
near Richmond.

Milton Barrett described Seven Pines in a letter home on
June 7.

Camps near Richmond　　　　　　　　*June the 7th 1862*
Dear brother and sister

　hit is with pleeasure that i take my pen in hand to let you
know that i am well hoping thes hasty rote lines may find
you injoying the same like blessing. i have went thru two
days battle and a weeks burning saft for whitch i feal very
thankful. on last saturday the 31 day of may we was orderd
to the chickakoma swamp. gen. Longstreets divishion was
all ready ingage with the emney. at one oclock our brigade was call into action and order to sport those brigade
that was all ready closely ingage. we was doble quick from
piont to piont and the yankees a playing on us with ther
shels and graps but forshnately non of our regiment got
kild but sevrel wonded. a heavy rain had fel on friday night
and the swamp full of water. we had to waid some places
waist deep. we routed the yankees from ever pershion tha
took except one battery tha retaken after gen. Hattres fell.[9]
we capture 26 peces of artilar two hundred barels of whiskey milatary stoers and so forth. the fight lasted tel dark.
we haven purcesion of the yankees camps and had drove
them back three mile. we lay in a line of battle all night
and had like to frese being so wet and hot all day. i never
suferd moar in my than i did that night. i was tiard wet
cold and Hungry. we move all of the wonded we could find
tha was some that had bin taken off by the yankees earley
a sunday moring. gen Longstreets actack the emney and
soon the battle wos fursley a ragin. we wos on Longstreets
left to keep them from flanking him. tha throw the shels

and graps in a bonance a mong us but we noble helt our ground. the firing lasted four hours when we drove them back and tha did not raley no moar. we gain a complete victor over them.

i can not give a true account of the loss for i do not know but i saw thousands of dead as i went over the battle ground.[10] the loss was heavy on boath sides but the yankees mutch the grates. Hamptons Liegons suferd ceverley and many others reg los wos heavy. we left the battle ground a sunday even and stade on the out post til last night. we was releve and fel back a few mile to rest. we expect a nother fight soon.

i must close for the wont of paper.

your effecnate brother
MILTON BARRETT

Jesse and caroline Mcmahan

The "thousands of dead" referred to by Milton became an all-too-common occurrence. The staggering losses in frontal assaults suffered by both Confederate and Federal forces are in part explained by battle conduct. Infantry usually fought shoulder to shoulder, in two parallel lines, prepared to fire to the front or the rear. This approach, premised on the use of a muzzle-loading smooth bore musket, emphasized offensive tactics. The introduction of the long-range repeating rifle just before the war, however, provided the defense with a powerful advantage against frontal assaults.[11] The failure of both Union and Confederate commanders to adjust to this change in part explains the high level of casualties.

On May 31 General Joseph E. Johnston was wounded,

and on June 1 General Robert E. Lee was appointed the
new commander of the Army of Northern Virginia. General
Lee completely reorganized the army. Hood's command was
placed in a two-brigade division under Brigadier General
William H. C. Whiting, and Whiting's own brigade was
now commanded by Colonel Evander McIvor Law of the
Fourth Alabama. Following Seven Pines, Hood's Texas Brigade was augmented by the addition of Hampton's Legion.

In his definitive study of the Texas Brigade, historian
Harold B. Simpson notes what was to come for the brigade: "It was fortunate that the three Texas regiments were
brigaded with such renowned fighting units as the Eighteenth Georgia Infantry and the foot companies of Hampton's Legion. Hood's Texas Brigade was to receive its sever-
est test of sustained battle action during the summer of 1862.
It was to engage in a blood bath from which it would never
fully recover—Gaines' Mill in June, Second Manassas in
August, and Antietam in September, three of the hardest
fought battles of the war." [12]

The Seven Days battle, from June 25 to July 1, produced
some of the bloodiest fighting of the war and largely consisted of offensive attacks by Lee against the numerically su-
perior Army of the Potomac led by General George McClellan. The deadliest encounter, at Gaines' Mill, represented
the first great triumph of Hood's Brigade.

As part of a maneuver of deception by Robert E. Lee,
Hood's and Law's brigades were to join Major General
Thomas Jonathan ("Stonewall") Jackson and were to attack
Federal forces isolated north of the Chickahominy. The plan
did not fully materialize, but on June 27 Hood led his bri-
gade against strongly fortified Union positions at Gaines'
Mill, following unsuccessful Confederate assaults by other

units. Hood, personally leading the Fourth Texas and the Eighteenth Georgia, broke through the Federal lines in a bayonet charge and established a breach that was subsequently exploited in heavy fighting.

Although Hood's Brigade as a whole earned its reputation as a fighting force that day, it was clear that the Fourth Texas and the Eighteenth Georgia were at the forefront. Unfortunately the casualty figures emphasized this. The Fourth Texas suffered 44 killed, 208 wounded, and 1 missing. Losses in other regiments were comparatively few, except for the Eighteenth Georgia. Milton Barrett's unit had 14 killed, 128 wounded, and 3 missing.

Hood's Brigade saw only limited action during the remainder of the Seven Days battle and then enjoyed a month of rest and recuperation near Richmond. There is no evidence that Milton Barrett saw his wounded brother Benjamin at Chimborazo Hospital in Richmond before Benjamin died, but we can certainly hope that he did so.

On July 26 Brigadier General Whiting was granted medical leave. He never returned, and Hood took his place as commander of the division, initially only temporarily. Wofford replaced Hood in charge of the Texas Brigade, although he was not promoted to brigadier general until April 23, 1863, to rank from January 17, 1863. Lieutenant Colonel S. Z. Ruff assumed command of the Eighteenth Georgia.[13] Ruff was elected colonel on April 23, 1863, also to rank from January 17, 1863. He was killed at Knoxville on November 29, 1863.

On August 8, 1862, the Texas Brigade, as part of Major General James Longstreet's command, left camp and began a period marked by almost continuous fighting and marching that lasted until late September. Robert E. Lee pushed northward against the forces of bombastic Major General John Pope, in command of the Union Army of Virginia. Longstreet's men kept Pope occupied along the Rappahannock while Stonewall Jackson outflanked the Federal army and on August 26 destroyed Union supplies at Manassas Junction in the Yankee rear. The Confederates had achieved a stunning tactical success, but the two Confederate forces were widely separated by an intervening Federal army.

On August 26 Longstreet's men began a fatiguing forced march to join Jackson. The Texas Brigade, led by Hood, reached Jackson on August 29, when Jackson's troops were strongly engaged by Pope's legions. As Harold Simpson states, "Napoleon had never directed a better maneuver than Lee did at Second Manassas. After dividing his army to gain both tactical surprise and position, Lee reunited his two forces on the battlefield, thus confronting the Federals with his maximum strength." [14]

Hood's Brigade was involved in a brief but severe encounter on August 29 but found glory—and bloodshed—on August 30. After the overconfident Pope committed almost all his reserves against the beleaguered Jackson, Longstreet launched a crushing flank attack against the unsuspecting Federal forces between 4:00 and 4:30 in the afternoon. Hood, in his book *Advance and Retreat*, called the movements of Longstreet's divisions "the most beautiful battle scene I have ever beheld." [15] The Confederate army won a smashing victory, advancing almost two miles against the demoralized Federals.

The Eighteenth Georgia was in the thick of the mass advance, fighting generally as a compact unit. On August 30 the regiment, with the Fifth Texas and Hampton's Legion, captured most of the Fifth and Tenth New York regiments, taking a four-gun battery and the colors of the Tenth New York. Casualties in the Eighteenth Georgia were heavy, with 19 killed and 114 wounded; it lost, among others, three color-bearers.

After only one day's rest, Hood's sadly reduced brigade began its march in Lee's invasion of the North on September 1. The Texas Brigade crossed the Potomac at White's Ford on September 5. It then camped for several days beginning September 7, approximately three miles south of Frederick on the banks of the Monacacy River.

Maryland Frederick   *Sept. 9, 1862*
Dear Brother and Sister,

These lines leaves me well hoping thes haisty rote lines may find you all well. i am very mutch fatige by hard marching and fighting. i have bin in two big battle Scence i rote and has march sevrel 100 miles. we hav gaind victore after victore and has advance sevrel miles in this state, has capture sevrel railroads and has cut off them from the western states. every thing is plenty and cheap hear but it wont stay so long. Maryland is a joining our army as fast as tha can. no dout that we will git 50000 in this state.

This is a butiful cuntry with rich valeys and lofty moutians. tha rase large a mount of hay and grain and the pepel appears true to the southren cose. i dont know wher our next movement will be but supose to Baltimore.

i have not heard from non of you in some time. we have not got no mail scence we left Culpeper. tha say we will git our mail in a few days. Our regiment lost 152 in the battle of manasas, 17 dead on the field and sevrel has dide scence. the first battle that we was in was on the 29 of Aug. our loss was light on that day. we charge them and run them one mile. we slade sevrel hundred and on the 30 the bigest battle was fought that has bin fought in this campaine. Hampton's legon fought on our right and the 5 Texas on our left. We all suffer a heavy loss. Our reinforcements was sloe a giting to us. We went so fast tha could not keep up. We was relive by the 18th S.C. and gen Evins command other divishins suferd equal to ours. i am no ida how many was in gage. our reg. and the Legon and the 5 Texas kild ten to wher we got one kild and we took sevral peces of artilar. our regt. took 4 peces on the same hil wher I just [illegible].

Write to me. direct your letters to Richmone til i order you to chang. i will git your letters soone or later. Give my best respect to all inquiring frend.

i am your loving Brother.   MILTON BARRETT
Jesse McMahan

After passing through Frederick, Hood's Division joined the remainder of Longstreet's command in its march to Boonsboro on September 10, passed through Hagerstown, Maryland, on September 13, and fought in a quick skirmish before dark on the fourteenth at the battle of Boonsboro, or South Mountain. During the night of the fourteenth, Hood's Division marched west to Sharpsburg, near Antietam Creek, and arrived there at noon on September 15.

The battle of Antietam resulted in the bloodiest single day of the war. The Texas Brigade, including the Eighteenth Georgia, was again in the center of the struggle, as part of Hood's small division of two thousand effectives. After artillery exchanges, the battle was in fact opened by the Eighteenth Georgia in front of the Dunker Church on the evening of September 16. This engagement in the East Woods and Miller's Cornfield, which foreshadowed the much larger confrontation of the seventeenth, was the only Confederate action on September 16.

The extraordinary bloodletting known as Antietam began early on September 17. At about 7:00 A.M., Hood's division began its successful drive against the Federals from Miller's Cornfield in front of the Dunker Church, but the fighting was among the bloodiest of the war. Attack and counterattack blended in fury. The Texas Brigade was not relieved until 10:00 A.M. The weary men then retreated to their previous night's camp to regroup. Although the brigade did not see further battle action on September 17, it did remain on the line from noon until 4:00 P.M., positioned near the church to defend in case of further attack. The Texas Brigade spent the evening of the seventeenth just north of Sharpsburg.

Casualties on September 17 were 23,000, with McClellan suffering about 12,500, and Lee 10,500. Almost half the casualties were incurred in the Cornfield and immediately adjacent areas. The Texas Brigade was virtually eliminated as a fighting force; 560 were killed, wounded, and missing out of its entering force of 854. This 66-percent casualty rate was, according to historian William F. Fox in his study of battle losses, the third highest in percentage losses for a brigade in a single battle. The Eighteenth Georgia had 13 killed, 72 wounded, and 16 missing, for 101 total casualties out of 176 men in the battle. Colonel S. Z. Ruff of the Eighteenth wrote in his official report that all of his men and officers acted with the "most desperate coolness and gallantry [and] not one showed any disposition, notwithstanding their terrible loss, to fall back or flinch from the enemy until they received orders to do so." [16]

A correspondent for the *New York Herald* reported the Texas Brigade's actions in Miller's Cornfield as follows: "That those ragged, filthy, wretched, sick, hungry and in all ways miserable men . . . should prove such heroes in the fight, is past explanation. Men never fought better. There was one regiment . . . that stood up before the fire of two or three of our long range batteries and two regiments of infantry and though the air was focal with the whistle of bullets and the screams of shells there they stood and delivered their fire in perfect order." [17]

The brigade's performance at Antietam did not go unnoticed by the Confederate command. In a letter to Senator Wigfall on September 21, 1862, General Lee wrote, "They have fought grandly, nobly, and we must have more of them. . . . With a few more such regiments as those which Hood now has, as an example of daring and bravery I could feel much more confident of the results of the campaign." [18]

Antietam was, of course, a bloody stalemate, but after its conclusion the Confederates withdrew across the Potomac into Virginia. The Union's success at Antietam in halting the Rebel drive into the North had long-term significance, since it provided the base on which Lincoln could issue the Emancipation Proclamation.

In late September and through most of the fall of 1862, the Texas Brigade recuperated in the Old Dominion. But the Eighteenth Georgia and Hampton's Legion were not to continue as part of the brigade. In November the Army of Northern Virginia was reorganized by states. The Eighteenth Georgia was accordingly transferred on November 26 from Hood's Brigade to the brigade of Brigadier General

Confederate dead at Dunker Church, Antietam, September 1862
(Courtesy of the Library of Congress)

Thomas Reade Rootes Cobb, of Georgia. Cobb's Brigade was in the division of Major General Lafayette McLaws, also of Georgia, in the First Corps, Army of Northern Virginia, still under the command of General Longstreet.

In his farewell order to the Eighteenth Georgia on November 27, General Hood referred to the regiment as one that had "shown itself unsurpassed for gallantry." In a warmer tone, Hood described the loss of the Eighteenth Georgia in his memoirs: "Under the unfortunate organization of brigades by States, I lost the Eighteenth Georgia and Hampton's Legion, to both of which commands, I, as well as my Texas troops, had become warmly attached. The former had served with me longer than the latter, and in every emergency had proved itself bold and trusty; it styled itself, from a feeling of brotherhood, the Third Texas." [19]

The Eighteenth Georgia suffered during this period many of the logistical difficulties that then confronted the Confederate army. In addition to a shortage of arms, the Eighteenth Georgia lacked clothes and shoes, a problem that had afflicted most of the Army of Northern Virginia during Lee's invasion of the North in September. In November 1862 Milton's regiment alone was reported to have 160 barefooted men, out of a brigade total of 440.

The maneuvering between the Federal and Confederate forces accelerated after Major General Ambrose E. Burnside replaced General George McClellan on November 9, 1862, as commander of the Army of the Potomac. Burnside, who is better known today for his sideburns than his military leadership, decided to move against Lee. The battle of Fredericksburg occurred on December 13, 1862, when Union forces under Burnside assaulted heavily fortified Confederate positions. The result was a Federal disaster, leading

Robert E. Lee to make his now-famous remark, "It is well that war is so terrible. We should grow too fond of it." The Union suffered 12,653 casualties, compared with Confederate losses of 5,300.

The Eighteenth Georgia was again in the very center of the battle, manning the famed stone wall at the "sunken road," approximately four hundred yards above the Fredericksburg city limits. Cobb's Brigade, consisting entirely of Georgians, held this sunken highway at the base of Marye's Hill against a series of futile Yankee charges. General Cobb was killed during the third Federal charge, just as Brigadier General Joseph B. Kershaw brought up two South Carolina regiments in support. The Eighteenth Georgia suffered 11 killed and 47 wounded out of the 235 casualties in Cobb's Brigade.

> *December 16, 1862*
> *Fredericksburg, Va.*

I am proud I can inform you of another victory against the Yankees on the 13th. The battle began at daylight and lasted till dark. Our brigade was engaged all day. Our regiment shot 200 rounds. This is the ninth fight I have been in. I was litter bearer and could not have protection of the entrenchments. I never did a harder days work in my life.

> Your loving brother,
> MILTON BARRETT

Letter to Caroline Barrett McMahan

Following Cobb's death, Wofford took over the brigade and was promoted to brigadier general to rank from January 17, 1863. Wofford's Brigade continued to serve in the division of Major General McLaws in Longstreet's Corps. During the winter of 1862–63, the divisions of generals McLaws and R. H. Anderson defended the road from Chancellorsville to Spotsylvania.

Milton wrote a letter from Fredericksburg at the end of January, in which he again referred to the battle of December 13.

Headquarters camp near Fredericksburg, Va.

January the 28th, 1863

Dear Brother and Sister,   It is with pleasure that I take my pen in hand to let you know that i am well hoping when these lines come to hand that they will find you enjoying the Same life's blessing. I have nothing interesting to wright that is nothing worth noting occurd.

Scence the battle everything has bin still a long the line. each party ocupise the same ground they did before the battle. a flag of truce is sent all most day long and we exchange papers and all. The news has bin a float that the enemy was a Crossing the River above and be low but i think it is all stuf. They have bin a fixing a roade on the north side of the river like they aim to cross at Rockoon ford and they have bin a marching troops down the river like they was a going to cross at fort roal. i think this is done to draw our force a way from hear, then they would make another attempt to cross here. we are not abot to meet them at the places and not weaken this point. they are all ready a moven some troops in order to meet the emergenc if they should attempt to cross. We have given them the worst whipping that they have ever got. it was a sight to see the battlefield. the dead was a lying thick over a bout one hundred achors of ground and strange to tel but not les strange than true the heaps of the dead to make brest works to sight behind. tha was not but one third of our ingag heare for we did not nead them. i do not think that they can be something moar don this winter. We have had lots of rain and it is now a snowing as fast as it can allready four inches deep. Neather army can move til better weather.

I received your kind letter bearing date Jan 16. the contents give me grate pleasure to hear from you. Jenkins brigade is in two miles of us and the legon is with them. i saw some of them yesterday and he told me that Capt. Bowing had not got back yet.[20] I am a going down to see them in a few days. i gest i will git them things you sent me. you will except my thanks for the gloves, and Socks is the very thing i nead. i will close by asking you to write soon. i am your loving brother.

MILTON BARRETT

To Jesse and Caroline McMahan

THREE

Giting Tiard
of This Thing,
1863

After the completion of his twelve-month term of enlistment in April 1862, Lawrence Barrett decided not to reenlist. His discharge was dated June 1862.

The summer of 1862 could not have been a particularly happy time for Lawrence. As we have seen, his brother Benjamin died on August 2 at Chimborazo Hospital in Richmond. Sometime in 1862, his mother, Mary Bradley Barrett, also died.

On December 1, 1862, the sale of the estate of William Barrett was conducted. Among the purchasers were Jane Collett, Jesse McMahan, Benjamin Barrett's widow, Martha, and, principally, Lawrence Barrett. Total sales were $342.33.

During this period, the McMahans received their first letter from Laban Augustus Mauldin, a neighbor of the McMahans and Barretts. Laban Mauldin was born on February 6, 1842, the son of Vardrey and Mary Dacus Mauldin. He enlisted in the Confederate army on June 12, 1861, in Columbia, South Carolina, for twelve months' service. He was in Company D, the "Gist Rifles" of Hampton's Legion, which was mobilized in Columbia by Captain Henry J. Smith.

The eight infantry companies of Hampton's Legion were made part of Hood's Texas Brigade in early June 1862 and fought with the Texas Brigade at Second Manassas, South Mountain, and Antietam. (Hampton's Legion was originally organized on June 12, 1861, by Wade Hampton, allegedly the richest man in South Carolina and subsequently governor of the state.) Laban Mauldin thus presumably fought with Milton Barrett when both the Eighteenth Georgia and Hampton's Legion were with Hood.

In mid-November 1862, as part of the reorganization of the Army of Northern Virginia by states, Hampton's Legion was assigned to the brigade of Brigadier General Micah Jenkins. Jenkins (1835–64), of Edisto Island, South Carolina, fought as colonel of the Fifth South Carolina at First Manassas and later formed the Palmetto Sharpshooters in April 1862. Promoted to brigadier general on July 22, 1862, he was wounded at Second Manassas. He arrived at Chickamauga just after the battle, and he participated in the Knoxville Campaign. Jenkins was regarded as one of the most promising of the young Confederate generals when he was killed by the accidental fire of Confederate soldiers at the battle of the Wilderness.

The letters written by Laban, and those written by Lawrence, in 1863 reflect malaise and discouragement. The effects of the war were becoming clear.

> *Hampton Legion*
> *Camp near Frederick*
> *Feb 4th, '63*

Dear friend

I received your kind letter. I was glad to hear that you & family was well. These few lines leve me well & I do hope these few lines may reach your distant hand in dew time &

find you & family well & enjoying all the pleashers of life.

I have nothing very interesting to write. I sopose fighting Joe Hooker, as he is called, is in command of the Yankees here & I hear he says he intends to fight the rebbles where ever he finds them. I think he had better change it a little & say he will have to fight the rebbles where ever he comes upon them.

I feel confident that he cant stay where he is no longer than the weather is inpassable for an army for if he dont do something by the time the good weather sets in General Lee will, & when he moves there will be something done.

You speak something of peace being made this year. Oh if peace only could be made soon I could not express my joy, for I tell you I am ageting tired of such a life as this (I mean peace favorable to the Confederacy I never will be willing to except peace otherwise). I see nothing much to induce me to believe peace will be made yet awhile although I hear of parties in the north But I dont think they are split up enough to bring peace yet a while. They are oblige to get Sick & tired of this war, or chastised some way or other before they will make peace.

Jesse I do want to see you and your family mity bad. I have not forgotten all the pleasher that I have seen with you all. Oh such times is passed & gon I am a fraid forever. If I only could get to stay one night with you all I think it would be more enjoyment to me than all the times my [illegible] from you has been.

There is nothing more but Sorrows & trubles to be Seen. Oh I will be glad when it is gods will to restore Peace to our unhapy & distressed country. tell James that I received a letter from him today & that I will answer it in a day or so.

The health of our army is tolerable good at this time. I think I have as good health now as ever I had in my life.

Give my love & respects to all & except the same. I will close hoping to hear from you Soon.

I am as ever

L. MAULDIN

Direct your next letters in the care of Captain J. K. McNeely Company (D)

Lawrence Barrett did not enjoy a long sojourn at home. On May 3, 1863, he was conscripted into the army. Lawrence joined Laban Mauldin in Hampton's Legion, serving as a private in Company I, one of the two infantry companies previously added to the original eight to bring the legion to regimental strength.

Following Lawrence Barrett's conscription, his letters primarily reflect his concern about his family's situation and the risks of Confederate service. His comments are both plaintive and pessimistic.

Franklin Depot, Va.   *May 29th, 1863*
Mr. Jesse McMahan
Dear brothin in law   I availe myself of the opportunity of droping you a few lines to inform you that I am still in the land of the living. my health is in decline. I truly hope these lines may reach you in due time and find you and family well. I have no war nuse to write. it has become disgusting to me to write it. I rote to you some two weeks ago and hav not got any answer as yet. I rote to you concerning my business & in hope that you will take it in hand. I think

it will be to your own interest as life is so uncertain and Death is sure. I want you to make sure to save your self.

I want you to let me no how they are amanageing business at home. I want to do a good part for them and at the same time I want them to do a good part for them selves that is to be saving of what they hav. I left $20 at home and I will send money to you as I get it and you can let bud [presumably his brother John Henry Barrett] have it as you see if he needs it or time advances. I will write what else I would like for you to do for me. that account against the estate and several other papers is in Janes ceare. you can get them at any time. you can concider your self my lawful agent whatever you see cause to do with anything it is rite with me.

I got a letter from Milt the 15th he was well giving me a long account of the late fredricksburg fight. 106 killed and wounded in his regt. 14 dead on the feild. write soon as I am ancious to heare from you. prospect crops and co.

W. L. BARRETT

Laban Mauldin wrote to the McMahans from Virginia in June.

Hampton Legion
South Quay, Va.
June 5, 1863

Dear friend,

I received your kind letter yesterday evening & was truly glad to hear from you & to know you all is well. These

few lines leves me well hoping they may reach your distant
hand in dew time & find you all well.

Jesse, I have nothing new or interesting to write. everything remains quiet.

Jesse, we are camped on black water river & we spend
a grate portion of our time in fishing & other sport in the
river which is veary amusing to soldiers.

I am truly glad to hear of such good prospects of fine
crops this year. if ever we needed fine crops it is now. we
must have subsistance from some whcre & if it isnt made in
the Confederacy I dont know how we will get it.

I would gladly healp you save your wheat but I am a away
here in the wilderness of Virginia & can do nothing but
stay here but maby there is a good day a coming if not our
hapyness is forever lost.

Give my love & best wishes to all of your brothers and
their family.

I will close hoping to hear from you again soon.

I remain your true friend & well wisher.

L. MAULDIN

To Jesse MacMahan & family.

Milton, meanwhile, had been at his post with Wofford's
Brigade. He sent home a series of letters in the winter and
spring of 1863.

Fredericksburg, Va.   *Feb. 21st 1863.*

Dear Brother and Sister, it is with pleasure that I embrace this opportunity of informing you that I am well, hoping these lines may reach you in due time and find you all enjoying the same like blessings.

Everything is still along the line, nothing of note has occurred since I wrote last.

Our regiment has just come off picket. We stood close together and could talk to each other, then when the officers were not present we exchanged papers and barter tobacco for coffee. The way we managed this is with a small boat. with sail set it will go over by itself then they send back in return the same way. Some of our boys went over and stayed awhile. The yankees would let us know when to come back. This correspondence has to be kept secret from the officers.

Gen. Longstreet's corps is moving. a large portion of it is on the march and we expect to march in a few days. I know not what parts they are going. Tha are marching toward Richmond, I suppose they aim to go to North Carolina. I hear that a large part of Hookers has gone there. Old Stone wall will take charge of this Post.

We have had a severe snow storm but night before last there came a warm rain and it all melted. Today is a pleasant day.

We have a variety of news and some indication of peace but I put little faith in peace being made soon. I dont see any probability of peace tho talk of the north western states seceding and joining the South. This would stop the war and shut up the eastern yankees right where they ought to be.

Our army never was in better fix for fighting than they

are now. The health of the army is excellent and our ranks
have been filled with conscripts and if we dont have to too
much we never can be whipped while we have such a leader
as General Lee.

The South Carolina Brigade is all left, I have seen but
very few of the boys since the battle. I saw John Stevens
a few weeks ago. We are all making out tolerably well;
we get short rations but can do very well on them. They
are paying us five dollars a month for to make up for our
rations.

I believe I have told you all that is worth telling. Give my
best respects to all inquiring friends and accept a portion
yourselves. I want to hear from you soon. I am your loving
brother

MILTON BARRETT

To Jesse and Caroline
McMahan

*Frederickburg va
March 11, 1863*

Dear Brother and sister

It is with pleasure that i take my pen in hand to inform
you that i am well hopeing thes lines may reach you in dew
time and find you all injoying the same like blessing. i receive your kind letter in dew time and the contents give me
grate pleasure to hear that you was all wel. we have had a
bunence of bad weather. it snow all day yestday but it has
all melted today and the sun a shining very perty. Tha is
but very litle news a float now. every thing on our line is
still a waiting a few fair days to put the roads in good order
for a hard attack.

As the spring makes its approach we are thretin with dark clouds that is a risen in the west and south and north of turable storms that is a threatin our young republick and two months will bring a grate change over our land and if we are sucseful at the three points now threaten by the enemy our sucess is shore and wil bring a speady end of this wicket war so let us be of good cheer and pray for success. Jinkins Brigade has left hear. it is in camp near petersburg so i wil not see J. B. King. But the socks and gloves wil not be lost for if i dont git them some other poor fellow wil that needs them worst per haps than i.

So far i have met with the good luck to git sutch things tolrable easy. Some of our boys has jest come from home and brong 17 large boxes of provishon. one of my mess-mates was fortinate enuf to git a large box of ham sausage and butter and other sweetmeats. So we have had a fine breakfast and has enuf to do us sevrel days. two moar started home on furlows. we draw to see who would go first. i come out blank a gain. i can not tel when i wil git to go home. two wil go ever month tel we all git off.

Scence i commence writing i hear some firing up the river but it is very sloe and i think it is the calvary at the forde.

Times is a shuting in perty tite hear. meat is a giting perty carse. we git ¼ of a pound per day. beef has plade out. we git a litle sugar that use to sweetin our tea with. we ar tolrable wel.

Col wofferd is our Brigdier gen and Ruff our Col. Capt. O'Neill has resign and Lieutenant Lemon wil be our capt.[1] i dont like this Brigade as wel as i did texas.

i am your loving brother

MILTON BARRETT

Fredericksburg va   *April 14th 1863*
Dear Brother and sister

A duren the past week the grates angsity have prevail
owing to the fairs at charlston allmost breathles silents.[2]
i have read the telegrams of the day and find all right so
far. But i have no idea that the enemy wil stop at the weak
effort tha have made on the citty But will vigurs renew. A
nothing of particlar note have occurde in this porshun of
the army. tha have bin some litle crumishing between the
calvery But of no importence. Last week tha was a con-
sidrable stur a mong the yankees in front of our line and
a considerable fireing a going on and is reported by a lady
that come thrue by a flag of truce that some regiments had
lade down ther arms and started home and that tha was
a gard out to arest them and a fight took place But i put
litle faith in this report. I think tha was a practicing or else
ther offers had reported victore at charleston and tha was a
firing saluts to tha success.

The enemy is a filling up ther army with Draffed men
as three hundred thousand of ther times will expiar the
first day of May But i suppose tha will be prest in And we
will have a powful army to contend with this summer. it
is all a humbug a bout them a laying down ther arms and
going home in spite of hier athority. tha ar under as good
disciplan as our army And ours cannot lay down ther arms
and go when ther terms of in list ment is out. Tha is not as
good fealing a mong the troops as mite be. tha all a giting
tiard of this thing call war.

Some ten days ago a grate visit took place at Richmond.
a bout one thousand women arm ther self with axes and
clubs and firearms and march in to the citty and broak
open stoers grocers and comassary's took what every tha

Confederate fortifications at Marye's Heights, Fredericksburg, Virginia, May 1863 (Courtesy of the Library of Congress)

wanted in spite of milatary or sivel authority. Jeff Davis got among them to make a spheech But could not stop them in this case tel he give them what tha wanted. ther was women that live in the serverbs of the citty and the head leders was wimen that ther husmen was imployed in the government shop at ten Dollars per Day and tha have bin sevrel men arested that have bin caught a pedling on articles that was taken that day. Our newpapers have bin very cearful not to say anything a bout it But i see the yankees have got a full history of it by exchange prisnors.[3] The fack is to wel known to be disputed that we ar a runing short of suplyes and if what we have on hand will do tel the new crop come in and thar is a sefishent suplies of grain made tha will be meat for the cattle nor hogs is not in the cuntry. we git no beef now and not quite half rashons of bacon and some times it is spoilt so we cant eat it. we git a plenty of flour. the cearsity of provishons is a cosing a grate deal of uneasi-ness a mong the soldiers. the yankees cant whip us only by starving us out.

The weather have bin pleasent for sevral days. we heave preaching ever Sunday by our chapel the revrent Mr. Dool of Maryland who was sign to our regiment when we first come to va and he have don much good in tending on our sic and wounded and seeing that tha was proprly tended to. he has all ways bin in the battle field ready to do his part in cearing for the wounded and have spair no pains at the hospital in seeing that tha was all promply tended to. he is of the Meathis faith.

Theas lines leaves me in good health hoping tha thes lines may come to hand in dew time and find you all wel. i will close hopeing to hear from you soon. i am your loving Brother.   MILTON BARRETT

To Caroline and Jesse McMahon

Milton's mention of the Reverend Mr. Dool was a timely one. During the spring of 1863 the first of several religious revivals swept over Confederate camps. In the first two years of the war the efforts of the Confederate army's chaplains were more or less unsuccessful. By 1863, however, religion took greater hold, for several reasons advanced by Bell Wiley. He suggests that the initial reaction in the camps against religion had been only temporary and that in 1863 soldiers were merely returning to the strong religious traditions in which they had been reared. Wiley also suggests that the initial optimism among troops and among the Confederate population at large had begun to fade. Certainly Milton Barrett's statement on April 14, 1863, rings true: "tha all a giting tiard of this thing call war."

As Milton Barrett mentioned in his letter, a chaplain's duties varied, but they most frequently consisted of preaching and caring for the sick and wounded. Often the chaplain was responsible for contacting the families of the sick and dead in any given regiment or brigade, while some chaplains even took on the role of teaching soldiers how to read and write.

The battle of Chancellorsville, regarded by many as Lee's greatest victory, took place from May 1 to May 4. Lee, with approximately 60,000 men, attacked and defeated General Joseph Hooker's army of 130,000 soldiers. McLaws's Division, including the Eighteenth Georgia, remained with Lee and provided the basic line of defense against the Federal army while Stonewall Jackson made his famous flank march and attack on May 2. On Sunday, May 3, as the Federal lines retreated, the divisions of McLaws and Anderson moved to meet Jackson's Corps. In his official report, McLaws noted that his orders were to hold his position on May 2 and not to engage seriously, but to press strongly as soon as it was discovered that Jackson had attacked. Wofford's Brigade became "seriously engaged" on May 2 after the advance was ordered in support of Jackson's attack. McLaws referred to the significant role of Wofford's Brigade on May 3 as follows: "General Wofford threw a portion of his command across the valley between him and the Chancellorsville heights and thus prevented the escape of a considerable body of the enemy which had been opposed to his brigade and to his left and front during the morning. I directed a flag of truce to be sent them and they surrendered. I think that General Wofford is entitled to the most credit for their capture." [4]

After the battle of Chancellorsville General Lee reorganized his Army of Northern Virginia. The Eighteenth Georgia, led by Colonel S. Z. Ruff, was in Wofford's Brigade, still in McLaws's Division. The army now consisted of three corps with three divisions each and four brigades in each division (except three divisions that had five brigades each).

On June 8, 1863, Milton Barrett was transferred from the Eighteenth Georgia to Company E, Third Battalion, Georgia Sharpshooters. The Third Battallion, Georgia Sharpshooters, was formed in May 1863 almost entirely from units in Wofford's Brigade. Each company was to be composed of fifty men to facilitate quick manuevering. The men were drawn from the larger existing companies. (Wofford noted on April 24, 1863, that of his four largest companies, Milton's Company A had eighty-six men.) Leading the Third Battalion was Nathan L. Hutchins, Jr., who joined Company I (the Hutchins Guards) of the Sixteenth Georgia Regiment in 1861 as captain. He was elected lieutenant colonel of the battalion. The Third Battalion, Georgia Sharpshooters, was attached to Wofford's Brigade, so

Milton Barrett remained with his comrades of the Eighteenth Georgia. At about the same time, on June 1, 1863, Milton was promoted to third corporal.

On Wednesday, June 3, Lee's army began its second invasion of the North. The plan was to march through the Shenandoah Valley and on to Pennsylvania to attack the Union army on its own ground. McLaws's Division began from Fredericksburg on the third, and other divisions started out on the fourth and the fifth from various locations. Milton wrote the McMahans from Winchester, Virginia.

Camps on the banks of the Shannado ten miles of

winchester va june the 22th 1863

Dear Brother and sister,   i take my pen in han to let you that i am well hopeing thes lines may find you all well. I was at Culpeper when I rote last. we havc bin a marching every scence a round an thrue the blue ridge from place to place as surcomstances requierd. our Divishon have not bin in no fight yet. tha have bin a right smart of fighing in this vicinity but no big battle. i have saw a grate many prisnors that our troops have captured within the last week. fighing Joe [Hooker] ar a retreating and Gen Ewel have captured Millroals hole force.[5] we are in pershession of winchester and Martinsburg and harpers fery and Maryland hights and Manassas Gap. we have got olde Joe in a bad box.

we have had very warm weathe and dry til the last few days. we have had rain in abounce and have lay the dust and the roads is very wet. we waided the river last night. it was up to our arms and it was with much difacult that we keep our provishons and powder dry. several of the boys fel down and got ther rashons and powder wet. we are a lying over hear to day a resting and i thought i would write you a few lines for i dont know when i will have the oppertunity of wrighing a gain. it is thought that we will be the invaders be fore long. i beleve i have told you all that is worth teling.

I have not heard from Laurence in some time. we have got our Battalion orginise at last. hereafter you will address me as folring (Richmond va McLaws Divishon wofferds Brigade Co. F S.S. Batt). we ar a giting a plenty to eat hear now and i dont think we will have much fighing to do this side of the Potomack. i will close for the present.

i am your loving Brother   MILTON BARRETT
To Jesse
   and
   Caroline Mcmahon

From June 19 to June 22, Longstreet's First Corps faced some skirmishing along the Blue Ridge Mountains, and on June 23 the corps marched to the Potomac, crossing at Williamsport. After meeting the Third Corps at Hagerstown, Maryland, the First Corps marched to Chambersburg, Pennsylvania, where they spent two days, from June 27 to June 29. By the evening of June 30 most of the First Corps, including McLaws's Division, was camped near Chambersburg, about twenty-four miles from Gettysburg.

At the end of the day on July 1, McLaws received orders to march to Gettysburg. His division marched all night, stopping to rest only two hours. At sunrise on July 2 the division arrived at Marsh Run, four miles from Gettysburg, and rested.

The battle of Gettysburg is appropriately viewed as the great battle of the Civil War. Unfortunately we have no direct record of what role Milton Barrett played in the battle. No letters have survived.

The only day on which Wofford's Brigade was significantly involved was July 2. Although official reports do not disclose much information about the role of Wofford's Brigade, it does appear clear that the brigade played a critical and timely role in the Confederate successes of July 2. Longstreet had only two of his three divisions in action on July 2, since the division led by Major General George Edward Pickett had not yet arrived in Gettysburg. McLaws's Division was deployed on the left of Longstreet's line, next to Hood's Division. The divisions were in two lines, with the brigades of Paul Jones Semmes and Wofford behind Kershaw's Brigade. In the famous fighting for the Peach Orchard and Little Round Top, Wofford's Brigade was in reserve, while Hood and the brigades of Semmes and Kershaw took the lead. With Longstreet riding with Wofford, Wofford's Brigade joined the charge, the Confederates taking the Peach Orchard and the Wheat Field and moving toward Little Round Top. Losses for Wofford's Brigade at Gettysburg were listed as 30 killed, 192 wounded, and 112 missing.

Following the battle, Wofford's Brigade withdrew to Virginia, leaving Gettysburg on July 5. The brigade was attacked at Chester Gap near Manassas on July 20, but by August 3 it was camped on the south side of the Rapidan River.

Lawrence Barrett's company was stationed near Petersburg, Virginia, in July and August 1863 and did not participate in the battle of Gettysburg. Indeed, Edward Porter Alexander noted that Jenkins's "big South Carolina brigade had been kept below Petersburg for nine months and . . . had little fighting since Sharpsburg."[6] The letters from Lawrence reflect his discouragement and his concern for his family.

Camp Neare Richmond   *July 18, 1863*
Mr. Jesse McMahan   I againe embrace the opportunity of droping you a few lines to inform you how I am doing. my health is some better than it was the first month after I got here. it is now bad enough. I have nothing in the way of nuse to write only the papers say that Lee is back in Va. I hav never heard from Milton since they left Culpepper. John Mauldin got here on the 15th and delivered the letters and other tricks in good order all of which I very thankfully recd.[7] I suppose that you hav a bundance of raine in that country. it is the same way here. the wheat is in the field yet but I dont think it is mutch hurt. they stack ther wheat instead of shocking it.

I will say to you that I want you to do as I requested of you. you know that life is uncertaine in the best of health and in case that I should die I want what is there to pay for itself all though I hope that with what I can send to you in time that the debt can be paid without braking up the family at home. tell Washington to write to me and give me his views upon the political affares and I will respond to it accordingly.[8]

the soldiers has a by word when any body dies or anything lost saying its gone up the spout. tell Washington that I say the Confederacy is on her way up the spout. nothing more.

W. L. BARRETT

As reflected in his letters, Lawrence's health was not good. The muster rolls for Company I at this time, now at the National Archives, show Lawrence as "sick in camps."

The discouragement evidenced in Lawrence's letters was not unique. The South Carolina Unionist B. F. Perry, who had earlier unsuccessfully sought in his native Greenville to stem secession fever, was distressed by the Confederate failures at Gettysburg and Vicksburg. William Francis Guess wrote, "The same news so afflicted B. F. Perry in Greenville that he stopped writing in his Journal. He told his wife that his heart was broken. His last entry gloomed that 'whether restored to the Union . . . or held as conquered Provinces we are a ruined people!' But Perry's was an angry despair. He was indignant for the 'poor men from the mountains,' drafted to bleed in a hateful cause while the plutocrats who 'urged on the contest' were happily profiteering at home. He cried 'Shame! Shame! on the farmers & planters . . . now asking four or five dollars per bushel for corn & seven & eight for wheat.'" [9]

William Collett's stay on the coast of South Carolina ended in early May 1863. On May 4 the Confederate government ordered Beauregard at Charleston to send five thousand men to Mississippi as soon as possible as reinforcements for the defense of that state and the relief of Lieutenant General John Clifford Pemberton. On the same day, General Beauregard assigned the Sixteenth and Twenty-fourth South Carolina regiments, as well as other units, to a new brigade to be commanded by Brigadier General States Rights Gist. Gist (1831–64) was a graduate of South Carolina College and Harvard University Law School. Despite his education in Massachusetts, his political views followed his name. A volunteer aide to General Bee at First Manassas, he was appointed brigadier general in the provincial Confederate army in March 1862. An able soldier, General Gist was killed at the battle of Franklin on November 30, 1864, as were fifty-five other soldiers from the Sixteenth South Carolina infantry.[10]

The Sixteenth Regiment, now part of the Department of Mississippi and Louisiana, left for Mississippi soon after May 4 but arrived too late to participate in the skirmish and evacuation of Jackson on May 14, 1863.

Mississippi
July 24, 1863
Dear Sister

I take the preasent opportunity of droping you a few lines to inform you that theas few lines leaves me Well hoping when theas few lines come to hand Will finde you Well and injoying you Self fine. I have went threw A heap of Narow esscapes since I have bine out her. the bulets and shel have sailed a Rowound me thick but not one didnt hit me at tall.

I come of Remarcable Well for the Way the balls fell a Round me. We have fell back from Jackson thirty five miles. i think that we Wil come back to South carolina in a short time, that is the talk in hour Rigement that We will leave in a few days for Charlston.

there Was a man shot out her the other day for deserten.

I want you to tell all of the children howdy for me and all in quiring friends. i wante you to tell Jane that Brown and Martin is Well, So i will come to close for the time by saying fare Well for thime.

W. A. COLLETT

To Caroline MacMahon

The Sixteenth South Carolina Regiment did not, in fact, return to Charleston as Collett had predicted. It formed part of General Joseph E. Johnston's force, which unsuccessfully attempted to relieve pressure on General Pemberton's Confederate forces soon under siege at Vicksburg. During the period from May 20 to July 20, General Johnston's army, which numbered slightly fewer than thirty thousand men, engaged in a series of marches and countermarches. Johnston chose not to attack General Ulysses S. Grant but failed to extricate General Pemberton. Following the surrender of Vicksburg, General Johnston withdrew his forces to Morton, Mississippi, in mid-July.

The disasters of Gettysburg and Vicksburg were followed by more bad news for the Confederates: the brilliant advance of Major General William Starke Rosecrans through Tennessee culminated in the Confederate evacuation of Chattanooga on September 8. Confederate president Jefferson Davis, however, decided to counter this move by sending significant reinforcements to General Rosecrans's adversary, Confederate General Braxton Bragg, commander of the Army of Tennessee. These maneuvers in the West were to have the fortuitous result of reuniting many troops recruited from Pickens District, including Milton and Lawrence Barrett and William Collett.

Gist's Brigade, part of the division of Major General William Henry Talbot Walker, was encamped at Morton, Mississippi, from July 20 until late August. In response to Bragg's request for troops, two of Johnston's divisions, including Walker's, were ordered to join Bragg. General Gist's brigade was subsequently sent to Rome, Georgia, at the extreme left of Bragg's line on Chickamauga Creek.

In early September 1863 President Davis also decided to detach Longstreet's First Corps, which included both Jenkins's and Wofford's brigades, to Tennessee to aid General Bragg. On September 9 Longstreet's men left the Rapidan line and headed for Richmond. Because of recent Federal occupation of east Tennessee (Union troops under Burnside took Knoxville on September 2), Longstreet's Corps had to travel by way of North Carolina and Atlanta. McLaws's Division, with Hood's Division and Alexander's batteries, made the trip to Tennessee by train. The 843-mile trip took seven days and ten hours over sixteen different railroad lines with varying gauges, illustrating some of the logistical problems that consistently burdened the Confederacy.

Neither Milton nor Lawrence Barrett saw action at the battle of Chickamauga, since both Wofford's and Jenkins's brigades arrived after the battle on September 19–20. Longstreet with other units of his corps, however, spearheaded a Confederate victory. In less than two hours of battle at Chickamauga, Longstreet's available force lost almost 44 percent of its strength. The success was costly, with the Confederates suffering 2,389 killed and total casualties of 17,804.

William Collett also did not fight at Chickamauga. Although Gist's Brigade was in action on September 20, it participated without the Sixteenth Regiment, which with its light battery remained at Rome.

To the despair and anger of many of his subordinates, Bragg refused to pursue the defeated Federals after Chickamauga. Instead he decided to lay siege to the Yankees in Chattanooga.

During the following weeks, the Barrett brothers and other soldiers from up-country South Carolina were able to meet regularly. The Sixteenth Regiment, entirely from Greenville County, for the first time in the war was in the same theater as Jenkins's Brigade. Jenkins's Brigade now included not only Hampton's Legion but also Benjamin Barrett's former unit, the Second Regiment, Rifles, with its complement from Pickens District. Other South Carolina brigades—those of Joseph B. Kershaw and Arthur M. Manigault—were also in Tennessee.

Milton Barrett wrote two letters home from the area near Chattanooga, the first on September 24 and 25.

Sept the 24th 1863

On the Battlefield near Chattanooga Ten
Dear Brother and sister   I seit my self behind a bluff to pertect me from the Yankee bums that have bin a whirling a round us in grand stile this morning.

i have bin on the front line two days a poping a way. on last tuesday even we had a hard crurmish had several kild and wounded. we did not get hear in time to take a part in the battle last Sat and Sunday. i past over the Battle field last monday. it was a terable slauter. the dead lay thick for a bout three miles. the Yankees have made a stand hear at this place. the right of ther line rest on the lookout mountain and the left rest on the river. tha are strongly fortified hear and have all ready open two battles on us. we have no hight for battle. we will have to flank them by crossing the

rivor or fall back a few miles. i can not tel what our genreals aim to do but i am shore tha will take us thrue right.
Jinkins Brigade took ther place on the line last night. i have
not saw any of them yet.

the Yankees is advancen. i must lay down my pen and go
to shooting.

September the 25th   we had a lively time last night.
we had a heavy crurmishing for three hours. we drove
ther crurmishinges in and kill sevrel. we had non kild a
few wounde. every thing is quite this morning. our line of
Battle have move back a bout one mile and ar a fortifying.
we still hold the lines that we first establish. we will have
to fall back a few miles to drive the enemy out. Bragg is
not the genral that Lee is and the western army cant fight
like the virgina army. if genral Lee was hear he would have
had the yankees drove out of Tennesee.

these lines leves me well. i will close hopeing to hear
from you soon. i am a ever your loving Brother

MILTON BARRETT

To Jesse and Caroline McMahon

We have one letter from Lawrence during this period,
his last.

Tennessee Chattanooga   *October 18th, 1863*
Deare brother in law   I availe the present opportunity
of droping you a few lines to inform you that I am in tolerble good health at this time hoping these lines may find
you all well. I rec'd your letter yestaday and was glad to
heare from you. Milton and Collett was present when I

received your letter. They are well. I will say to you that this is a bad place for troops but the best land that I ever saw. I guess Milt was bee hind the bluff that I was huged up behind a big sycamore tree.

the Yankees throw shell accasionnaly in our camps and cripled one man yestaday 4 o clock p.m. enemy quite today the weather is very wet. I hav just come in off picket and feel very mutch fatigue having to ly in a pit of water two days and nights at a time.

Tell Washington that I rec'd his letter and will answer it when I get paper fit to write upon. if Mr. Nichols wants that wagon sell it to the best advantage. I will leave it to you what it is worth in the condition its in. you know better than I do, sell the wagon and any thing else there you see proper. I would like to keep my mare if the family needs her. there will bee twenty dollars due me the 1st of next month. if I get it I intend to send it to you the first chance and then you take the money and my account gainst the estate and make Jamerson credt it upon the note. R. E. Holcombe and W. J. King can prove my account if it neds any proof. Nothing more [illegible]. do the best you can for me and I will do the best I can for you.

I remaine yours as ever

W. L. BARRETT

Jesse McMahan

Milton Barrett wrote again from near Chattanooga, about two weeks after Lawrence's letter.

Chatnooga, Tenn.   *Nov. the third, 1863*
Dear Brother and sister,

I embrace the opport. of wrighting you a few lines that will in form you that i am not in good health But ar able to stay with my command. The water hear does not a gree with me and I have had the direar every scence i have bin hear and it have reduce me down rite smarte. Lawrence is pestered with the same. i saw him this morning. he was a giting rite fat before he took the Direar.

Times is a giting moar exciteable every day. On wendesday night last Jenkins Brigade had a heavy ingagement lost about three hundred kild and wounded. George Bradley was kild.[11] Capt. Bowing was wounded and two of his Brothers. Tha is caninadeing a going every day But i dont beleve that a general ingagement will come of hear. i beleve one or other of the partys have to fall back.

We have had a bounance of rain have wash a way some of our railroad bridges, makes it very difacult to git supplyes. hear in fack our rashings have bin of a infery kind every scence we have bin heare, mostley corn meal and it damage and our beef not very good and I dout haveing that long.

I have not saw Collet in eight or ten days. he was well. we have bin a moveing and changing about so fer the last week i have not learn where his Brigade is. We are clost to Jenkins Brigade.

I believe i have told you all of the news that is worth teling. I receive yours of 22nd and was glad to hear that you all was well and also receive Malinda's letter an will ancer it in a few days. Tha is but few fur lows give now and tha in espechel cases. i think i will git one this winter if i dont git well perty soon. i am a going to make a effort for a fur low for i dont believe i will git wel whil i have to drink this blue lime stone water. Tha is a grate meany it serves likc it dose me.

Lawrence was well pleas with this cuntry. Sead he beleve it was a going to cure him. Sead he had a notion of buying him a farm hear. i was with him a hour or two this morning. He sead nothing a bout buying a farm. i will close hopeing thes lines may find you all well. Give my best respects to inquiring friends an except a porshon your self.

i remain your loving Brother.

MILTON BARRETT

The shortage of rations described by Milton Barrett was a serious problem for Confederate troops, particularly during the latter half of the war. The typical Confederate diet consisted of corn meal and either salt pork or lean beef, in insufficient quantity and subject to irregular deliveries. During the summer, and only in areas where no troops had recently passed, the soldiers would forage for "wild greens." "Cush," the mainstay of their diet, was a type of corn meal or "pulverized, moldy corn bread" mixed with pork grease. The food that the soldiers did have was often old, and weevils were frequently found in peas. As most of the soldiers' diet typically consisted of rice, wheat, maize, and tubers, there was little vitamin A available, which resulted, among other things, in night blindness.[12]

Milton and Lawrence Barrett remained in camp near

Chattanooga until November 4, 1863. Longstreet was then detailed with twelve thousand men of McLaws's and Hood's divisions, the latter of which was commanded by Micah Jenkins following Hood's severe wounding at Chickamauga, to east Tennessee to confront Burnside at Knoxville. On November 17 McLaws's Division arrived at the suburbs of Knoxville and engaged the Union army in various skirmishes.

The major battle for Knoxville—the assault on Fort Sanders—was fought on November 29. Wofford's and Benjamin G. Humphreys's brigades from McLaws's Division were assigned the task, with a third from Jenkins's in support. The three thousand Confederates overwhelmingly outnumbered the Yankees, but on half-frozen ground and encountering looped telegraph wire and strong resistance, they were soon repulsed. The Third Battalion of Sharpshooters kept the enemy under cover at the start of the assault. Confederate casualties were heavy—129 killed, 458 wounded, and 226 captured—particularly in contrast with the Union forces, which lost, out of fewer than five hundred soldiers, only eight killed and five wounded. Colonel S. Z. Ruff, leading Wofford's Brigade, was among those killed in the assault.

On December 3 Longstreet decided to give up the siege of Knoxville, largely because of reports that Major General William T. Sherman would be moving against him, following the Union breakthrough at Missionary Ridge. Longstreet moved his army east and north to Greenville, Tennessee, where he would be in position either to rejoin Lee in Virginia or to undertake operations in the West.

While Milton and Lawrence Barrett moved east with

Longstreet, William Collett and the Sixteenth South Carolina Regiment were posted on Missionary Ridge above
Chattanooga. Gist's Brigade joined in the retreat after the
Federal success at Missionary Ridge on November 25 and
spent the winter months near Dalton, Georgia.

FOUR

He Will Suffer
No More,
1864

The unhappy culmination of the war for the Barretts was to occur in 1864. We have few letters from this period, but extant records are sufficiently revealing.

As the year opened, William Collett was in north Georgia, and Milton and Lawrence Barrett were in east Tennessee. That winter was the coldest of the war. From the last few days of 1863 until the middle of January 1864 the temperature hovered around zero degrees Fahrenheit in east Tennessee. The troops faced a serious shortage of food and clothing. At one point, according to Longstreet, the soldiers were even using raw beef hides to protect their feet from the frozen ground, until the railroad opened and brought a shipment of three thousand shoes. Longstreet wrote, however, that "the men were brave, steady, patient. Occasionally they called pretty loudly for *parched corn*, but always in a bright, merry mood. . . . At this distance it seems almost incredible that we got along as we did, but all were then so healthy and strong that we did not feel severely our really great hardships." [1]

Milton Barrett was on leave for eight days, his furlough expiring in early February 1864. On February 22, Longstreet's Corps left its winter quarters and began its march

up the Holston River in east Tennessee. By April 1 much of
the corps was encamped near Bristol.

Camp near Bristol, Tenn.   *April 1st, 1864*
Dear Brother and sister,

I avail myself with the oppertunity of writing you a few
lines that will inform you that I am injoying good health
hopeing thes lines may come to your hands in dew time
and find you all well.

I was at New market when I wrote to you abilding winter quarters. I flatterd my self with a long an pleasant rest
but was i sadly disapointed. i had jest completed my cabin
an sleep in it two nights when we got marching orders.
We march to greenvill, Tenn and Bivowac. The weather
was pleasant for the first ten days. we drill two hours a day
views and inspecking reaglar twice a week. we was a goin
order back to Bulls gap to meet the enemy. we was gon
four days when we learnt that tha was no enemy near. We
return to our Bivowac at Greenville. now the rain and snow
put a stop to all milataria exersise. we stood a round our
blazing fires a midst storms of snow and wind with thout
any shelter except some small tents we toat a long to sleep
under. We have to git down and crawl in them.

Last Tuesday was a week a go the snow fel til it was seven
inches deep in the time that i have bin speakin of. Tha curtail down our rashings to two thirds of a pound of flour not
bolted and ⅓ a pound of bacon. This cose grate dissadisfaction a mong the soldiers. in fack it was barley enuf for
one meal per day. Hungry will cose a man to do all most
any thing. Tha was severil depperdation committed on the

sittuzins property sutch as taken chickens and meat. The thing went on this way for several days, the men all hungry and mad. We all a greede to go to the genral and if he did not give us moar rashings to charge the comasary an take by force. He had us a extray days rashins ishued and got us all sorty pasafide. We could buy a little flour by going eight or ten miles after it.

Things went on this way til the 28th. we got orders to march. We started a Monday the 28th it a snowing as fast as every saw it. It melted as fast as it fell. The roads was very mudy and slipry made it very disagreable travling. We got to this place last night and is to wait hear for further orders. i have no idea how long we will stay hear nor wher we will go. Tha have ben a talk of mountain us but I dont beleve it will be dun. We all have tolrable good close and Shoes. Our close is a very corse material of a dingie white sent to us by the State of Georgia. We call them our Joe Brown close.[2] I mean the Georgia troops.
[Remainder lost]

On or about April 10, 1864, Longstreet's Corps was ordered to rejoin the Army of Northern Virginia stationed by the Rapidan River in Virginia. After several days of rest in Charlottesville, the troops arrived at the end of April at a camp near Gordonsville for a week of intense training. The week and month ended with several days of troop inspection by General Lee. New uniforms and shoes, as well as more food, had arrived from the quartermaster in time for the occasion.

During the following months both Lawrence Barrett and

William Collett died, although the exact circumstances are unclear.

Little is known of Lawrence Barrett after the events in Tennessee in 1863. Hampton's Legion muster rolls for September and October 1864 show that he was last paid on March 1, 1864, by Major Mauldin and that he had been taken "Prisoner of War." Family records, which cannot be substantiated, state that Lawrence was sent out on picket. A skirmish ensued, and Lawrence was never seen or heard from again. No Union records have been found regarding Lawrence's possible capture.

Gist's Brigade, including Collett's Sixteenth South Carolina Regiment, participated in Johnston's defensive campaign north of Atlanta in 1864. The brigade left its winter quarters on May 6 and engaged Federal forces at Resaca. It did not participate at New Hope Church. By June 19 the brigade was part of the defensive line at Kennesaw Mountain and remained there until early July. Major C. C. O'Neill of the Sixteenth was killed while on the picket line.

William Collett died while the Sixteenth Regiment was entrenched at Kennesaw Mountain. A privately printed history of the Sixteenth notes that Collett was killed at Kennesaw Mountain. Official records, however, disclose that he died on June 25 at Kingston Hospital. It seems reasonable to assume that he suffered mortal wounds at Kennesaw Mountain, but it is certainly possible that he died of other causes.

Meanwhile, Milton Barrett persevered with the Third Battalion, Sharpshooters, apparently participating with Wofford's Brigade in the battles of the Wilderness, Spotsylvania, and Cold Harbor. The battle of the Wilderness began on May 5, and although labeled a Confederate success, it resulted in heavy casualties. Almost immediately after the battle of the Wilderness, both armies began marching south to Spotsylvania Court House. Wofford's Brigade was one of the units in the First Corps, which reached Spotsylvania Court House ahead of the Federals on May 8. The two armies began combat on the afternoon of May 8 and continued to fight at Spotsylvania until May 21. The Confederate victory at Spotsylvania was followed by another on the North Anna River from May 23 to May 26. The Confederates continued to keep Grant and his men away from Richmond by inflicting heavy casualties at Cold Harbor, from May 31 to June 12.

Wofford's Brigade continued to move with Lee's Army of Northern Virginia in the defensive effort to shield Richmond. It was from the banks of the James River near Petersburg that Milton Barrett wrote his last letter to the McMahans that survived the war. The letter that appears here was transcribed from a copy of Milton's letter, not the original, and the copyist apparently "improved" Milton's spelling, grammar, and punctuation.

Camp on the south side of the James River, Va.
August 1, 1864
Dear Brother and Sister,

I embrace the opportunity of writing you to let you know that I am still numbered among the live and in good health. Hoping these lines may find you all in good health, and surrounded with enough of this world's goods to make life comfortable. I received your letter of the 14 of July in due time, and was glad to hear from you. At the same time I regret to hear of the death of Tom Collett, and do deeply

sympathize with a bereaved sister and will offer her a word
of consolation. Your husband is gone to a world of rest
where there is no tumult of war. The keen sounds of the
fifes and the long roll of the drum will not summon him
to his post, nor the roaring cannon break him of his rest.
He will suffer no more hunger nor thirst, so Dear Sister,
grieve not at your loss, for your loss is his gains. He died an
honorable death: he gave his life, a sacrifice for his country's rights. May peace and happiness be with you are the
sincere wishes of your brother.

Since I wrote to you last there have been some active
movements of the army. I suppose you have heard of them
so I will confine myself to what has come under my own
observation. General Earley has made a very successful
raid in Maryland, and in Pennsylvania gained a victory and
brought off a number of horses, beef cattle and military
stores. Also destroyed a great deal of railroad. Our division left Petersburg ten days ago and went to Chaifeng
Bluff on the north side of the James River. The enemy had
crossed over with one army corps and was a threatening
to storm that place which would give them an opening to
Richmond. We spent several days there a scouting around
to find the enemy's position. On the morning of the 28th,
we attacked them near Melvin Hill. A brisk fight took place
for about three hours. We drove them at first. They fell
back to their strong position when General Kershaw withdrew his troops. The loss was not very great on either side.
I do not know the number. On the evening of the 29th
General Kershaw with three divisions renewed the attack.
We found that the enemy had evacuated the fortification.
Our battalion was deployed as [illegible] and a batt. from
Kershaw's brigade. We advanced about one mile when we

Camp Winder

Confederate States of America.

Richmond Oct 14 Day

1861.

Dear Brother and Sister thrue
the kind provadents of and all wise god i am
enjoying good health while many of my Brother
Solgers has sickeen and dide hoping thes lines
may find you all well i have nothing that will
interrest you mutch to write we hear a plenty of news
but a litle that i can put confadents in we will
git a dispatch one day and the next hit will
contredicted we heard some time a go that our
army had crost the potomie but hit is not
so but hit will have to be crost before the
city can be taken for to march men to the
tenth lighths would be foley we will have
to force them out by strubing them an
cuting them of from other so els'plise
we are still a minding our yankees in ther
cage i beleve i told you in my letter that
we wos a garden the prisnors about 2000
we have bin a garden them are month an
an has to gard them a nother we have sent
five 100 to new orleans but tha git no
less tha are like the widers oil tha send
in moar ou less evry weak

Above: Letter from Milton Barrett
Right: Letter from Lawrence Barrett, written on ledger paper

Oct 18th 1863

Tennessee Chattanooga

Dear brother in law I availe the present opportunity of dropeing you a few lines to inform you that I am in tolerble good health at this time hopeing these lines may find you all well I recd your letter yesterday and was glad to heare from you Milton and collett was present when I received your letter they are well I will say to you that this is a bad place for troops but the best land that I ever saw I guess it but the Milt was behind the bluff that I was huged up behind a big sycamore tree the yankes throw shell accasionaly in our camps and cripled one man yesterday 4 oclock P M every quite to day the weather is very wet I hav just come in off picket and feel very much fatigue haveing to ly in a pit of water two days and the parts at a time

Assistant Commissary.

came up on their pickets. A lively skirmish fight took place. It was as hot as I ever was in for a few minutes. It gradually died away, and dark put a stop to the combat. We had a few men wounded, none killed, in our battallion. The same day, the yankees all left Petersburg, except a small force, and crossed to the north side of the James. We were within a few hundred yards, and we could hear them a crossing back to the south side. We reported it to headquarters early the next morning. We continued our pursuit toward the landing. We passed through the camps that they had just left. They had left almost everything. They had tried to destroy their plunder. They had cut up their blankets and clothes, and had left their breakfast on the fire. Some had potatoes, some chicken and butter, all of which they had taken from the citizens — to which our boys done full jestice.

We soon got in sight of the landing and saw that all had left but a few that garrison there, and some gunboats on the river.

We stopped within six hundred yards of their works. Thought they would not shell a skirmish line. We put out a few videttes to watch, and the rest of us went to the shades, a helping ourselves to such things as they had left. There was abundance of meat and hard bread, and lots of other tricks. One man found five hundred and seventy dollars of greenbacks. Then they let in to shelling us from their gunboats. We got inside the fortification and lay low for a while.

Col. Hutchin of our battallion, got a very bad wound in the shoulder, but, I am glad to learn, it is not a mortal wound.[3] Another one of our boys got a fatal wound.

We marched the same night to this place. My feet are blistered till I can hardly walk today.

Grant thought he had Lee, but he got beat at his own tricks. He dashed his troops over the river, a threatening Richmond, to get our troops withdrew from Petersburg, and tried to dash back and take it. But Gen. Lee was wide awake. Grant had tunneled under our fortifications in order to blow us up and take Petersburg. He let off his blast, and blew up one hundred and fifty yards of our works which was occupied by the 18th Regiment of South Carolina. He killed and wounded thirty two. He charged with his Nigro Troops that come yealing like Devels, crying, "No quarters." They got to the works. Our troops charged them, got back to the works, killed five hundred negroes and took two prisoners and set them to work.

We took 1,000 white troops. I don't know what our loss was but it was pretty heavy, but nothing like the enemy's. The 18th and 17th loss heavy. I forgot to tell you that we took two regts. of Yankees in the fight that I have mentioned. I don't know what they numbered.

      I am your loving Brother MILTON BARRETT
To Jesse and Caroline McMahan

The battle of the Crater on July 30 was one of the more notorious events of the war. The imagination and skill involved in tunneling under Confederate lines came to tragic naught for Federal forces, as muddled Union troops went into the Crater instead of around it and became sitting ducks for regrouping Confederates. Yankee casualties numbered 4,000; Confederate casualties totaled 1,500.

Blacks had served in both the revolutionary war and the War of 1812, but it was not until after the Emancipation Proclamation took effect on January 1, 1863, that black soldiers were officially allowed to enlist in the Union army. Unofficially, however, blacks from several large Northern cities had volunteered in the Union army before 1863 and had been serving in the Union navy since the beginning of the Civil War, primarily as firemen, coal heavers, cooks, and stewards. In the late summer of 1864 President Lincoln reported that there were approximately 130,000 black soldiers and sailors fighting in the Union army.[4]

The stalemate at Petersburg led to a series of movements in the Shenandoah Valley. In early August Grant increased the strength of the Army of the Shenandoah. On August 6 Lee and Jefferson Davis decided to send additional troops to Lieutenant General Jubal A. Early in the Shenandoah in order to counter the threatening Union buildup. Among the units to be sent to Early was Major General Joseph B. Kershaw's 3,500-man infantry division, of which Wofford's Brigade was then a part. By Sunday, August 14, most of the division was near Front Royal in the Luray Valley.

The Third Battalion, Georgia Sharpshooters, had just begun to participate in these operations in the Shenandoah Valley when Milton Barrett was captured on August 16. In the *Official Records of the Union and Confederate Armies*, an excerpt from the diary of the First Corps, Army of Northern Virginia, describes the manner in which Milton Barrett was probably captured:

> August 16—(Around 12 noon information was received that four brigades of the enemy's cavalry was on its way to Cedarville). To hold Guard Hill and cover the passage of the Shenandoah, Wofford's Brigade of infantry and Wickham's of cavalry and artillery are sent to seize the position, which is done with the loss of but eight or ten men. Wofford, however, moves off to the right to attack the enemy's cavalry, which had now come up in force, and just at that moment, having charged and driven

back our own cavalry, pitches into Wofford and drives him back in confusion and with loss. Brigade is subsequently moved across the river.[5]

Major General Philip H. Sheridan of the Union army described the same incident in a letter written on August 17 to Major General Henry W. Halleck, chief of staff, in Washington, D.C. Sheridan wrote that the enemy suffered the loss of two stands of colors, as well as 24 officers and 276 men captured: "Most of the prisoners are from Longstreet's corps and Kershaw's division. They came across the mountains from Culpeper, and report large reenforcements from Lee's army arriving. The cavalry made some handsome saber charges, in which most of the prisoners were captured."[6]

A fellow soldier of Milton Barrett's informed the family of Barrett's capture.

Camp near New Market, Va.   *1864*
                                         Oct. 11

Mrs. McMahan,

I Received a letter you wrote your Brother. I thought I would let you know What had become of him. He was taken Prisoner at Front Royal, Va. on the 16th day of August. He was not hurt as I now of. Your letter you Wrote to him was dated on the 29th Sept. I am sorry to say to you that he was captured. He was a good soldier and was always at his Post both in camp and in the time of battle.

I have not now war news to write you that will interest you only I hope we will whip the Yankees so that we will have peace this winter that is what I hope. The weather is getting very cold in the Valley. I hope the fighting is over in the Valley.

Elmira Prison, Elmira, New York, Fall 1864
(Courtesy of the Library of Congress)

I hope you Will write back if you get this letter. I done this to accomodate you and let you now about your Brother Milton. I Wil Close for the Present. I remain your friend with respects.

J. B. L. WALL

To Mrs. Caroline McMahon
Direct your letter as you did to your Brother
J. B. L. Wall[7]

Following his capture, Milton was first imprisoned at Old Capitol Prison in Washington, D.C., and then at Elmira, New York. Union records show that he was committed at Old Capitol on August 21, 1864, and sent to Elmira on August 28.

Elmira Prison was opened in Elmira, New York, in July 1864. Like a number of other Northern (and Southern) prisons, it was established exclusively for enlisted men. "No compound struck a deeper chill into the hearts of Confederate soldiers," according to one source. A Texan inmate at Elmira Prison wrote, "If there was a hell on earth, Elmira prison was that hell."[8] The prison stretched across thirty acres of land along the Chemung River in New York. The river often flooded, creating a stagnant pool forty feet wide and three to five feet deep in the center of the prison compound. Thousands of gallons of camp sewage were dumped into the pool. Regardless of the health hazard the pool presented, the manager of the camp did not arrange for prisoners to build their own drainage ditches until they had lived with the stench for several months.

Although the camp managers had been told that over ten thousand Confederate prisoners might be assigned to

Elmira Prison, the camp was built with barracks to hold merely half that number. Only six weeks after the prison opened, 9,600 Confederate soldiers were crammed into the prison, forced to sleep in temporary canvas tents or out in the open for want of sufficient barracks space.

By the winter of 1864–65, many prisoners had no blankets and insufficient clothing, and there was only one stove per barracks, to warm two hundred prisoners. In less than one year, 12,122 Confederates were imprisoned at Elmira; of these, 2,917 died in camp.[9] Ten prisoners died each day, on average. James McPherson points out that the highest death rate in a Northern prison was 24 percent at Elmira.[10]

Although Milton Barrett survived many of the major battles of the war, he did not survive conditions at Elmira Prison. He died of variola (smallpox) on February 12, 1865, and is buried in Grave 2108 at the cemetery by the prison.

Epilogue

The toll of the Civil War was staggering for both North and South. There are no certain statistics, only educated guesses. The distinguished historian Shelby Foote concludes that the North suffered 640,000 casualties out of a total of 2,000,000 soldiers and sailors, and the South had casualties of 450,000 in its force of 750,000.

	Federal	Confederate
Personnel	2,000,000	750,000
Killed in battle	110,000	94,000
Death from disease or mishap	255,000	162,000
Wounded	275,000	194,000

Source: Foote, 3:1040.

For the South, the burden of defeat was exacerbated by the loss of a particularly high percentage of its manpower. Most observers estimate that one of every four white Southern males of military age died in the war.

The writers of the letters in this volume reflect such human waste. Of the seven soldiers represented, only two, Laban Mauldin and J. B. L. Wall, are known to have survived the war. A corporal by September 1864, Laban Mauldin was paroled at Appomattox on April 9, 1865. He subsequently married Mary Amanda Rogers, lived in Easley, South Carolina, and died on August 10, 1915. J. B. L. Wall was procuring rations in Virginia when the war ended, and he died in Atlanta on May 26, 1929. Although we lose track of Jasper Strickland in 1861, records show a Jasper W. Strickland on an April 17, 1864, roll as a private in (New) Company H, First Alabama Regiment, at Fort Gaines, Alabama. He was paroled on May 16, 1865, in Montgomery, Alabama. This may or may not have been the admirer of Malinda Barrett.

As for the Barrett family itself, three brothers and one brother-in-law died. The different ways in which these soldiers died represent Confederate losses in general: Milton died in prison in 1865, Benjamin succumbed to battle wounds in 1862, Lawrence was missing in action and was probably killed in the battles of May 1864, and William Collett fell prey to wounds or disease in 1864.

The effects of the war on the Barrett family of Pickens District were no less severe than for the Confederacy as a whole. In 1859, when William Barrett died, his nine children were living, as was his widow, Mary. Ten years later, in 1869, the probate of the estate of William Barrett was concluded. The farm of one hundred acres was sold for $3,050 at a public auction on May 1, 1869, to Sarah Jane Barrett Hamilton, former wife of William Collett. Of the nine children living in 1859, only five were still alive. Three of the four sons were dead. Milton and Lawrence Barrett had left no descendants, and Benjamin Barrett's widow, Martha, had moved to Georgia with the couple's four sons. Only John Henry Barrett, born in 1849, survived. John Henry married Amanda Boswell, moved to Alabama sometime after 1880, and had at least one child, Elsie.

Among William Barrett's daughters, Rebecca Emeline died in 1866, and her husband, James McCoy, died before 1869, leaving four young children. Mary Ann, married to

John Powers, lived in Spartanburg County, South Carolina, and died in 1892 or 1893. Sarah Jane, widow of William Collett, married William Hamilton before 1869. After his death she married Bloomer Merck. Sarah Jane and William Collett had one daughter, Mary; Sarah Jane had three children by her third husband: Lawrence, Texana, and Missouri Merck. She died in 1873. Malinda, the youngest daughter, married Joseph King in 1865. She died in 1871, and her husband died two years later.

Finally, Lucretia Caroline and her husband, Jesse McMahan, continued to live in the Georges Creek area of Pickens County until 1870, when they moved to Oconee County. They had nine children who lived to maturity. Lucretia Caroline died on June 23, 1895. Jesse McMahan lived to be ninety-two, dying on May 3, 1896. Jesse and Lucretia Caroline are both buried at Fairview Methodist Church in Oconee County. It is to the McMahans and their descendants that we owe thanks for having preserved the letters included in this book.

Notes

Introduction

1. Hahn, 53.
2. Ford, 221.
3. Ibid.
4. Ibid., 236.
5. Wallace, 693.
6. McPherson, *Battle Cry of Freedom*, 20.
7. Wiley, *Life of Johnny Reb*, 336.

Chapter 1: Goin to Fight the Yankees, 1861

1. Ford, 369.
2. Ibid., 372.
3. Rivers, 31.
4. This almost certainly overstates the degree of support. The Confederacy subsequently decreased the size of a company, and the total number of men must have included many (such as Lawrence Barrett) who served in different units at different times during the war.
5. Brigadier General Barnard Elliott Bee (1824–61) graduated from West Point in 1845. He resigned from the U.S. army on March 3, 1861, and was appointed brigadier general on June 17, 1861. He obtained fame by his words to his troops at First Manassas, "There is Jackson, standing like a stone wall." Bee was mortally wounded at the battle of First Manassas.
6. Reid, 11.

7. Ibid.

8. The role of the Fourth Regiment is summarized in *Confederate Military History*, vol. 5, *South Carolina*, as follows: "Two companies of the Fourth, thrown out as skirmishers in front of the stone bridge, fired the first gun of the battle early in the morning, and the regiment bore a glorious part in the battle which Evans fought for the first hour, and in the contest of the second hour maintained by Bee, Bartow and Evans" (25).

9. The Sixth Regiment, ordered to Virginia on July 10, 1861, was engaged at Dranesville under Brigadier General James Ewell Brown ("Jeb") Stuart on December 20, 1861. Subsequently it was brigaded under brigadier generals R. H. Anderson, Micah Jenkins, and John Bratton (its original colonel). The regiment reported 18 killed and 45 wounded at Dranesville. In April 1862 it consisted of 550 officers and men, 27 of whom were lost at Williamsburg. At the battle of Seven Pines the regiment lost over half of its 521 officers and men.

10. Colonel Francis Stebbins Bartow (1816–61), of Savannah, commanded the Oglethorpe Light Infantry and then the Eighth Georgia. He was killed leading a charge down Henry House Hill at the battle of First Manassas.

11. Captain J. B. O'Neill was the original captain of Company A, Eighteenth Georgia. He was wounded on August 30, 1862, at the battle of Second Manassas and resigned, disabled, on March 5, 1863.

12. This was George Washington Custis Lee, son of Robert E. Lee. George W. C. Lee had been detailed to temporary duty at Goldsboro, North Carolina, leaving engineering work on the Richmond defenses.

13. The storms described by Barrett did have a major effect on Federal forces. On October 29, a huge land and sea expedition commanded by Union general Thomas Sherman and Union flag officer Samuel Francis Du Pont left Hampton Roads for the Carolina coast and Port Royal, north of Savannah. The fleet, consisting of seventy-seven vessels and twelve thousand troops, was

the largest ever assembled by the United States to that time. The expedition encountered heavy gales off Cape Hatteras, suffering severely. See Long, 132.

14. James A. McMahan, born in 1844, was the son of Alexander and Jane McMahan, neighbors of the Barretts. He enlisted on October 24, 1861, with Benjamin Barrett and was described in service records as being seventeen years old, five feet nine and one-half inches tall, with blue eyes, fair hair, and a light complexion. He was wounded at the battle of Frayser's Farm on June 30, 1862, and was discharged on August 16, 1862, incapable of further duties. His wound was described as a gunshot wound in the shoulder.

15. William F. King, a neighbor of the Barretts, had three sons of military age in 1860: Robert F. (twenty-three), William (twenty-one), and John (sixteen). At least two appear to have enlisted in Company E on October 24, 1861. Robert F., a sergeant in 1861, was killed at Petersburg, Virginia, on June 20, 1864. John was wounded at Spotsylvania Court House on May 10, 1864, and was paroled at Appomattox.

16. John E. Archer, thirty years old when he joined the First Battalion, South Carolina cavalry, appears to have served in South Carolina throughout the war.

17. General Pierre Gustave Toutant Beauregard (1818–93) was in charge of Confederate forces at the fall of Fort Sumter and then was second in command to General Joseph E. Johnston at the battle of First Manassas. A brigadier general at the time of First Manassas, he was made a full general to rank from July 21, 1861. Beauregard succeeded to command of the western armies at Shiloh following the death in battle of General Albert Sidney Johnston and subsequently was transferred to South Carolina in charge of the defense of the South Carolina and Georgia coasts. He later served under Lee in Virginia and surrendered with Joseph E. Johnston in North Carolina.

18. Barrett may have been referring to the engagement at Dranesville, not far from Leesburg, referred to in n. 9 above. Jasper Strickland may have participated in the battle.

19. Both the Union and the Confederacy experimented with using balloons for aerial reconnaissance. The best-known of the balloonists was Thaddeus S. C. Lowe, who became attached, as a civilian, to the Union army in August 1861. Barrett presumably saw one of Lowe's balloons.

20. McMurry, 31.

Chapter 2: *The Dead Was A Lying Thick, 1862*

1. References to the Collett family are found in the 1790 census (Sarah Collett) and the 1820 census (Greene Collett) of Pendleton District, and in the 1830 census (Elizabeth Collett) of Greenville County.

2. The return address on Collett's letter dated January 16, 1862, suggests that Collett was with the Eleventh Regiment, but this appears to have been an error or a reference to a temporary posting.

3. John S. Taylor, 10–11.

4. *Report . . . of the Military*, 31.

5. *Confederate Military History* 5:101.

6. The battle of Shiloh was fought on April 6–7, 1862. Instead of the "glorious vicktor" mentioned by Milton, Shiloh was a major Confederate defeat. This report—and that later in this letter with respect to Beauregard's success—reflect the inaccuracy and wishful thinking that regularly marked army rumors.

7. *Confederate Military History* 5:40–41.

8. Information on Chimborazo is from Robertson, *Tenting To-night*, 97–98.

9. Brigadier General Robert H. Hatton, a native of Ohio, was commissioned colonel of the Seventh Tennessee on May 26, 1861. He was killed at the head of his brigade on May 31, 1862.

10. The battle of Seven Pines, or Fair Oaks, was indecisive. Confederate casualties were 980 killed, 4,749 wounded, and 405 missing, for a total of 6,134 casualties from a force of 42,000. Union forces suffered 790 killed, 3,594 wounded, and 647 missing or cap-

tured, for total casualties of 5,301, also out of 42,000 effective troops.

11. McWhiney and Jamieson, 48–49.

12. Simpson, *Hood's Texas Brigade: Lee's Grenadier Guard*, 108.

13. Lieutenant Colonel S. Z. Ruff was the original deputy to Colonel Wofford, with the same date of rank: April 25, 1861.

14. Simpson, *Hood's Texas Brigade: Lee's Grenadier Guard*, 143.

15. Hood, 37.

16. *War of the Rebellion: . . . Official Records*, ser. 1, vol. 19, pt. 1, p. 930. Hereinafter cited as *Official Records*.

17. Quoted in Simpson, *Hood's Texas Brigade: Lee's Grenadier Guard*, 179–80.

18. Quoted in McMurry, 61.

19. Hood, 46–47.

20. Milton Barrett referred to Captain "Bowing" both in this letter and one dated November 3, 1863, from "Chatnooga." Captain Bowing was almost certainly Robert E. Bowen, who joined Company E of the Second Regiment, Rifles, with Benjamin Barrett in October 1861. Robert E. Bowen, thirty-one years old in 1861, was initially a first lieutenant in Company E. He was promoted to captain on December 19, 1861, and lieutenant colonel on November 13, 1863. He became colonel of the Second Regiment, Rifles, on July 20, 1864, and was paroled at Appomattox.

Chapter 3: *Giting Tiard of This Thing, 1863*

1. James Lile Lemon was originally a second lieutenant in Company A. Promoted to first lieutenant on June 5, 1862, he became captain on March 5, 1863. He was captured at Knoxville on November 29, 1863, and paroled on June 12, 1865.

2. On April 7 Flag Officer Samuel Francis Du Pont entered Charleston Harbor. He unsuccessfully attacked Fort Sumter but remained in the area.

3. The so-called bread riot occurred in Richmond on April 2. Food shortages in urban areas and elsewhere in the South were

periodically acute. This riot was put down after intervention by President Davis and local police and militia.

4. *Confederate Soldier in the Civil War*, 154.

5. The battle of Second Winchester was fought on June 13–15, with the Second Corps of the Confederate Army of Northern Virginia under Lieutenant General Richard Stoddert Ewell soundly defeating the federal forces of Major General Robert Huston Milroy. The Confederates captured over four thousand men as well as twenty-three guns and large stores. Among those captured was First Sergeant (subsequently captain) Andrew Washburn of the Eighteenth Connecticut, the great-great-grandfather of coeditor Carolynn Heller.

6. Gallagher, 316.

7. This was presumably the John Mauldin who was a private with Company D, the "Gist Rifles," of Hampton's Legion. John Mauldin was killed at Wauhatchie, Tennessee, on October 28–29, 1863.

8. George Washington McMahan was the brother of Jesse McMahan. He married Emily Berry in 1848. Both Washington and Emily McMahan died in July 1879.

9. Guess, 238–39.

10. Following the battle of Franklin, the bodies of General Gist and three other generals remained overnight on the back verandah of Carnton, the home of Colonel and Mrs. John McGavock. Colonel and Mrs. McGavock were direct ancestors of the coeditors.

11. Milton Barrett was referring to a relatively rare night engagement on October 28–29. Jenkins's Brigade, now under the command of Colonel John Bratton, attacked Brigadier General John W. Geary's troops at Wauhatchie in Lookout Valley. Despite initial success, the Confederates withdrew with 34 killed, 305 wounded, and 69 missing. The Second Regiment, Rifles, under the command of Colonel Robert E. Bowen, was apparently in the center of the struggle.

Among those killed at Wauhatchie was Sergeant George W. Bradley, referred to as a "noble solder" in *Confederate Military History* 5:311. George Bradley was from Pickens District and was almost certainly a cousin of the Barretts. He enlisted at Pickensville on October 24, 1861, at age twenty-two, and joined Benjamin Barrett and others from Pickens District in Company E of the Second Regiment, Rifles. He was wounded in the thigh on June 27 (Gaines' Mill) or June 30 (Frayser's Farm), 1862, and was wounded again at Second Manassas on August 30, 1862.

12. Stevens, 131–43.

Chapter 4: He Will Suffer No More, 1864

1. Longstreet, 515.

2. Joseph E. Brown (1821–94), born in Pickens District, South Carolina, attended Yale Law School and was the war governor of Georgia. He was a firm believer in states' rights, even if that position led him to oppose Confederate government policies.

3. Lieutenant Colonel Nathan L. Hutchins suffered a shoulder wound on July 30, 1864, and subsequently received a forty-day furlough. Following his return to the army, he was captured at Sayler's Creek on April 6, 1865, but was released from prison at Johnson's Island on July 25, 1865.

4. McPherson, *Battle Cry of Freedom*, 563, 769.

5. *Official Records*, ser. 1, vol. 42, pt. 1, p. 873.

6. *Official Records*, ser. 1, vol. 43, pt. 1, p. 19.

7. John Beck Lafayette Wall (1844–1929) enlisted as a private on August 24, 1861, in Company E, Twenty-fourth Georgia Regiment (the Rabun Gap Riflemen), a unit of Wofford's Brigade. He was captured at Crampton's Gap, Maryland, on September 14, 1862, and exchanged on November 10, 1863. He was transferred to Company E, Third Battalion, Georgia Sharpshooters, on June 8, 1863.

8. Both quotations are from Robertson, *Tenting Tonight*, 128.

9. Faust, 241. Of the 214,000 Confederates imprisoned over the course of the war, approximately 26,000 (12 percent) died. On the Union side, of the 211,000 troops captured, 194,000 were imprisoned. Of those, 30,000 (15 percent) died. McPherson, *Ordeal by Fire*, 451.

10. McPherson, *Battle Cry of Freedom*, 797n.

Bibliography

Primary Sources

Caldwell, J. F. J. *The History of a Brigade of South Carolinians*. 1866. Reprint. Dayton, Ohio: Morningside Press, 1984.

Dickert, D. Augustus. *History of Kershaw's Brigade*. 1899. Reprint. Dayton, Ohio: Morningside Press, 1973.

Douglas, Henry Kyd. *I Rode with Stonewall*. Chapel Hill: University of North Carolina Press, 1940.

Gallagher, Gary W., ed. *Fighting for the Confederacy: The Personal Recollections of General Edward Porter Alexander*. Chapel Hill: University of North Carolina Press, 1989.

Hood, John Bell. *Advance and Retreat: Personal Experiences in the United States and Confederate States Armies*. New Orleans, 1880.

Lewis, Richard. *Camp Life of a Confederate Boy of Bratton's Brigade, Longstreet's Corps, CSA*. Charleston, S.C.: News and Courier Book Presses, 1883. Reprint. Gaithersburg, Md.: Butternut Press.

Longstreet, James. *From Manassas to Appomattox*. Philadelphia: J. B. Lippincott Co., 1896.

Miller, Francis T., ed. *The Photographic History of the Civil War*. 10 vols. New York: Review of Reviews Co., 1911.

Pendleton District, South Carolina. Deed Books C-476, H-113, H-122, H-355, R-523, R525. Anderson County Courthouse, Anderson, South Carolina.

Population of the United States in 1860. Washington, D.C.: Government Printing Office, 1864.

Reid, J. W. *History of the Fourth Regiment, South Carolina Volunteers*.

1891. Reprint. Dayton, Ohio: Morningside Press, 1975.

Report of the Chief of the Department of the Military of South Carolina to Governor Pickens. Columbia, S.C.: Charles P. Pelham, State Printer, 1862.

Taylor, Walter H. *General Lee: His Campaigns in Virginia, 1861–1865.* Brooklyn, N.Y.: Braunworth and Co., 1906.

Tower, R. Lockwood, ed. *A Carolinian Goes to War.* Columbia: University of South Carolina Press, 1983.

Townsend, George Alfred. *Rustics in Rebellion.* Chapel Hill: University of North Carolina Press, 1950.

United States Census, South Carolina, 1790, 1800, 1820, 1830, 1840, 1850, 1860.

The War of the Rebellion: A Compilation of the Official Records of the Union and Confederate Armies. 1893. Reprint. Gettysburg, Pa.: National Historical Society, 1972.

Secondary Sources

Barton, Michael. *Goodmen: The Character of Civil War Soldiers.* University Park: Pennsylvania State University Press, 1981.

Beringer, Richard E., Herman Hattaway, Archer Jones, and William N. Still, Jr. *Why the South Lost the Civil War.* Athens: University of Georgia Press, 1986.

Bowers, John. *Stonewall Jackson: Portrait of a Soldier.* New York: William Morrow and Co., 1989.

Bruce, Dickson B. *Violence and Culture in the Antebellum South.* Austin: University of Texas Press, 1979.

Buel, Clarence C., and Robert U. Johnson, eds. *Battles and Leaders of the Civil War.* 4 vols. New York: Century Co., 1888. Reprint. Secaucus, N.J.: Blue and Grey Press, 1982.

Catton, Bruce. *The Centennial History of the Civil War.* Vol. 1, *The Coming Fury.* Vol. 2, *Terrible Swift Sword.* Vol. 3, *Never Call Retreat.* Garden City, N.Y.: Doubleday, 1961–65.

Coddington, Edwin B. *The Gettysburg Campaign: A Study in Command.* New York: Charles Scribner's Sons, 1968.

Confederate Military History. Vol. 5, *South Carolina*. Atlanta, Ga.: Confederate Publishing Co., 1899.

Confederate Military History. Vol. 6, *Georgia*. Atlanta, Ga.: Confederate Publishing Co., 1899.

The Confederate Soldier in the Civil War. New York: Fairfax Press, 1977.

Crute, Joseph H., Jr. *Units of the Confederate States Army*. Midlothian, Va.: Derwent Books, 1987.

Davis, William C. *The Imperiled Union: 1861–1865*. Vol. 1, *The Deep Waters of the Proud*. Vol. 2, *Stand in the Day of Battle*. Garden City, N.Y.: Doubleday, 1982–83.

———, ed. *The Image of War, 1861–1865*. 6 vols. Garden City, N.Y.: Doubleday, 1981–84.

Faust, Patricia L., ed. *Historical Times Illustrated Encyclopedia of the Civil War*. New York: Harper and Row, 1986.

Foote, Shelby. *The Civil War: A Narrative*. 3 vols. New York: Random House, 1958–74.

Ford, Lacy K., Jr. *Origins of Southern Radicalism: The South Carolina Upcountry, 1800–1860*. New York: Oxford University Press, 1988.

Fox, William F. *Regimental Losses in the American Civil War, 1861–1865*. Albany, N.Y.: Albany Publishing Co., 1889.

Freehling, William W. *The Road to Disunion: Secessionists at Bay, 1776–1854*. New York: Oxford University Press, 1990.

Freeman, Douglas Southall. *Lee's Lieutenants: A Study in Command*. 3 vols. New York: Charles Scribner's Sons, 1942–44.

Grunder, Charles S., and Brandon H. Beck. *The Second Battle of Winchester, June 12–15, 1863*. Lynchburg, Va.: H. E. Howard, 1989.

Guess, William Francis. *South Carolina Annals of Pride and Protest*. New York: Harper and Brothers, 1960.

Hahn, Steven. *The Roots of Southern Populism*. New York: Oxford University Press, 1983.

Horn, Stanley F. *The Army of Tennessee*. Indianapolis: Bobbs-Merrill Co., 1941.

Jones, Terry L. *Lee's Tigers: The Louisiana Infantry in the Army of Northern Virginia*. Baton Rouge: Louisiana State University Press, 1987.

King, Alvy L. *Louis T. Wigfall: Southern Fire-Eater*. Baton Rouge: Louisiana State University Press, 1970.

Klein, Maury. *Edward Porter Alexander*. Athens: University of Georgia Press, 1971.

Linderman, Gerald F. *Embattled Courage: The Experience of Combat in the American Civil War*. New York: Free Press, 1987.

Long, E. B. *Civil War Day by Day: An Almanac, 1861–1865*. Garden City, N.Y.: Doubleday, 1971.

McDonough, James Lee. *Chattanooga: A Death Grip on the Confederacy*. Knoxville: University of Tennessee Press, 1984.

McFall, P. S. *It Happened in Pickens County*. Pickens, S.C.: Sentinel Press, 1959.

McMurry, Richard M. *John Bell Hood and the War for Southern Independence*. Lexington: University Press of Kentucky, 1982.

McPherson, James B. *Battle Cry of Freedom: The Civil War Era*. New York: Oxford University Press, 1988.

——. *Ordeal by Fire: The Civil War and Reconstruction*. New York: Alfred A. Knopf, 1982.

McWhiney, Grady, and Perry D. Jamieson. *Attack and Die: Civil War Military Tactics and the Southern Heritage*. University: University of Alabama Press, 1982.

Mitchell, Reid. *Civil War Soldiers: Their Expectations and Their Experiences*. New York: Simon and Schuster, 1988.

O'Connor, Richard. *Hood: Cavalier General*. New York: Prentice-Hall, 1949.

Phillips, Ulrich B. *Life and Labor in the Old South*. New York: Little, Brown and Co., 1929.

Pope, Thomas H. *History of Newberry County, South Carolina*. Vol. 1, *1749–1860*. Columbia: University of South Carolina Press, 1973.

Pullen, John J. *The Twentieth Maine, A Volunteer Regiment in the Civil War*. Philadelphia: J. B. Lippincott Co., 1957.

Richardson, James M. *History of Greenville, South Carolina*. Atlanta: A. H. Cawston, 1930.

Rivers, William James. *Account of Raising of Troops in South Carolina for State and Confederate Service, 1861–1865.* Columbia, S.C.: Bryan Printing Co., 1899.

Robertson, James I., Jr. *General A. P. Hill: The Story of a Confederate Warrior.* New York: Random House, 1987.

———. *Soldiers Blue and Gray.* Columbia, S.C.: University of South Carolina Press, 1988.

———. *The Stonewall Brigade.* Baton Rouge: Louisiana State University Press, 1963.

———. *Tenting Tonight: The Soldier's Life.* Alexandria, Va.: Books, Inc., 1984.

Sears, Stephen W. *George B. McClellan: The Young Napoleon.* New York: Ticknor and Fields, 1988.

———. *Landscape Turned Red: The Battle of Antietam.* New Haven, Conn.: Ticknor and Fields, 1983.

Simpson, Harold B. *Hood's Texas Brigade: A Compendium.* Hillsboro, Tex.: Hill Junior College Press, 1977.

———. *Hood's Texas Brigade: Lee's Grenadier Guard.* Waco, Tex.: Texian Press, 1970.

———. *Hood's Texas Brigade in Poetry and Song.* Hillsboro, Tex.: Hill Junior College Press, 1968.

Stevens, John K. "Hostages to Hunger: Nutritional Night Blindness in Confederate Armies." *Tennessee Historical Quarterly* 48, no. 3 (Fall 1989): 131–43.

Taylor, John S. *The Sixteenth South Carolina Regiment, CSA.* Privately printed, n.d.

Thomas, Emory M. *Bold Dragoon: The Life of J. E. B. Stuart.* New York: Harper and Row, 1986.

———. *The Confederate Nation, 1861–1865.* New York: Harper and Row, 1979.

Thomas, John P. *General Micah Jenkins, C.S.A.* Columbia, S.C.: State Co., 1903.

Wallace, David Duncan. *South Carolina: A Short History, 1520–1948.* Columbia: University of South Carolina Press, 1961.

Warner, Ezra J. *Generals in Blue.* Baton Rouge: Louisiana State

University Press, 1964.

——. *Generals in Gray*. Baton Rouge: Louisiana State University Press, 1959.

Wellman, Manly Wade. *Giant in Gray: A Biography of Wade Hampton of South Carolina*. New York: Charles Scribner's Sons, 1949.

Wert, Jeffry D. *From Winchester to Cedar Creek: The Shenandoah Campaign of 1864*. Carlisle, Pa.: South Mountain Press, 1987.

Wiley, Bell Irvin. *The Life of Billy Yank: The Common Soldier of the Union*. Indianapolis: Bobbs-Merrill Co., 1952.

——. *The Life of Johnny Reb: The Common Soldier of the Confederacy*. Indianapolis: Bobbs-Merrill Co., 1943.

——. *The Plain People of the Confederacy*. Gloucester, Mass.: Peter Smith, 1971.

Index